CREATIVE
HOMEOWNER®

design ideas for
Kitchens

CREATIVE HOMEOWNER®, Upper Saddle River, New Jersey

VP, Editorial Director: Timothy O. Bakke
Production Manager: Kimberly H. Vivas
Managing Editor: Fran Donegan
Senior Editor: Kathie Robitz
Editorial Assistants: Evan Lambert (Proofreading); Lauren Manoy (Photo Research)
Senior Designer: Glee Barre
Author: Susan Boyle Hillstrom
Photography (unless otherwise noted): Mark Samu
Cover Photographs: (*top*) Design: Jean Stoffer; (*bottom left*) courtesy of Bosch; (*bottom center*) Design: Delisle/Pascucci; (*bottom right*) courtesy of Sonoma Cast Stone
Inside Front Cover Photographs: Design: Paula Yedyank
Back Cover Photography: (*top*) Design: Delisle/Pascucci; (*bottom left*) Builder: Witt Construction; (*bottom center*) Mark Samu, courtesy of Hearst Magazines; (*bottom right*) courtesy of Wolf Appliance Co.
Inside Back Cover Photography: Design: Jean Stoffer
Cover Design: Glee Barre

Current Printing (last digit)
10 9 8 7 6 5 4 3 2 1

Printed in China

Design Ideas for Kitchens
Library of Congress Control Number: 2004113486
ISBN: 1-58011-218-8

CREATIVE HOMEOWNER®
A Division of Federal Marketing Corp.
24 Park Way
Upper Saddle River, NJ 07458
www.creativehomeowner.com

Dedication

To my father, Vilas J. Boyle, who got me started.

Acknowledgments

Many thanks to Kathie Robitz, the perfect editor, for being helpful, encouraging, smart, and funny. And to the art staff, senior designer, Glee Barre, and photo researcher, Lauren Manoy, who made a beautiful book. Thanks also to my husband, Roger Hillstrom, for providing encouragement, support—and dinner.

Contents

ABOVE Fabulous faucet shapes and finishes enhance kitchen style.

RIGHT A large window brings the outdoors into a kitchen and plays up the home's architectural character.

BELOW A custom hood liner matches the cabinetry and disguises the exhaust system.

Since prehistoric times when people gathered around fires in caves, the place where food is prepared has been designated as the heart of the home. Technological advances have made the kitchen of today a marvel of efficiency, but it still has that almost primitive appeal—it's the place that draws people together. Everyone wants to be there, especially with others—members of the household, extended family, friends, neighbors. As the experts are fond of saying, the kitchen is a "multipurpose room." More than just a laboratory for cooking and cleaning up, it's the new living room, dining room, family room, and

Introduction

even the home office all in one. Therefore, the creation of a kitchen is a complicated affair. You can't just pull up a rock closer to the fire in the cave—you need to define your style and juggle cabinets, appliances, surfaces, and lighting to create a room that meets your cooking and socializing needs, expresses your design sensibilities, and jibes with your budget. That's where *Design Ideas for Kitchens* comes in handy. Use it as a guide through the planning and designing process. Let the beautiful photographs and helpful information alert you to the latest kitchen trends and products—and inspire you with possibilities.

The kitchen is everybody's favorite room. No longer tucked away and closed off from the rest of the house, it is a front-and-center space where family and friends gather to cook, eat, and entertain. It's also become a designer room. Efficiency is important, of course, but today's kitchen has to look great, too. With some effort, and perhaps help from a professional, your new or remodeled kitchen can be everything you want it to be—a warm and welcoming room where you prepare meals efficiently, spend time with your family, sit quietly to plan your day, and entertain in style.

Start with a Plan

| designed for living | kitchen layouts |
| islands and peninsulas |
| eat-in kitchens |

Today's dream kitchen functions as the heart of the home, with facilities for cooking, eating, and entertaining. To see more of the kitchen at left, turn the page.

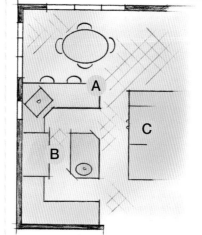

points of view

TOP LEFT Overall dimensions are generous in this multi-purpose space, but the food-preparation zone is defined by a compact and efficient peninsula that separates cooking and dining.

CENTER LEFT A favorite appliance of serious cooks, a pro-style range dominates the work area. The island supplies extra counter space and holds a second sink—a good design for two cooks.

BOTTOM LEFT The microwave and storage are placed away from the busy work area but handy to the dining space.

designed for living

Your dream kitchen will take some planning to meet the needs of your household. Find your focus in a family conference, discussing the new kitchen from each person's point of view. First, look at the kitchen you've got. What's good about it? What's not so good? Is it too small, too dark? Is storage lacking? Are the appliances old, the finishes faded? Have you always hated the cabinets?

Next, focus on the future. How will each family member use the new kitchen? Will everyone cook? Is this where the kids will hang out with their friends or do homework? Will you want a baking center, planning desk, dining area? Do you love to entertain? How sociable do you actually want to be? Will you chat with guests while you cook, or do you want to prepare your culinary masterpieces in private? Will you want to open your new kitchen to surrounding rooms or to the outdoors?

What about the size? Can you expand your present kitchen by annexing nearby space, thus avoiding major structural changes? Does your budget permit an addition? Perhaps just reconfiguring your present kitchen will do the trick.

Your family conference will produce a clear picture of the kitchen your family wants. Put the ideas you've discussed on paper in the form of a rough sketch. Whether you do the work yourself or turn the sketch over to a professional, you'll have taken the first step toward making your kitchen dreams a reality.

ABOVE A massive island devoted to both cooking and informal dining takes center stage in this streamlined kitchen.

LEFT The cleanup center is located across from the range, **RIGHT**, which includes two separate cooktops.

points of view

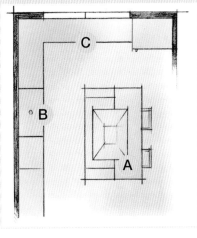

function times four

The massive multi-pur-pose island that dominates this space is a marvel of functionality, with a sink, a built-in microwave, storage, and an eating area. Stools can be tucked under the durable and glamorous granite top.

ABOVE LEFT All the elements of thoughtful design appear in this kitchen, starting with an up-to-date look of simplicity and warmth.

TOP Plentiful storage includes open shelves and drawers and cupboards in many handy sizes.

ABOVE Because undercounter storage is abundant, there are no wall units to detract from the clean and airy appearance.

RIGHT A narrow table is a handy drop-off place near the door for keys. It also keeps the phone and cookbooks within reach but away from the work area.

BELOW RIGHT The kitchen is large, but the space is arranged in tight and efficient work zones.

BELOW The counterspace is distributed so that there is an ample surface on either side of the range.

points of view

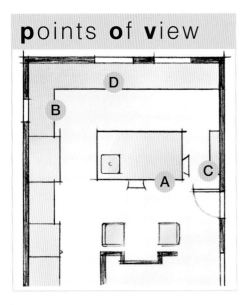

points of view

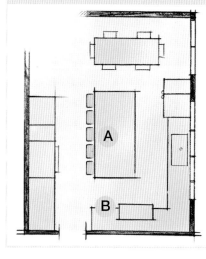

RIGHT In this spacious eat-in kitchen, family and friends can snack at the island counter or sit down to dinner at the far end of the room.

BELOW Here, the L-shaped layout is supplemented by the huge island, which accommodates both food preparation and eating.

design pros

what each pro knows

▌ **Architects** plan, design, and oversee new construction and major remodels. You will need one if your kitchen project involves an addition or an extensive makeover of existing space.

▌ **Certified Kitchen Designers (CKDs)** are schooled in all aspects of kitchen design, from layouts to equipment and materials to wiring and plumbing. Before choosing one, make sure your design sensibilities mesh.

▌ **Interior designers** can be of great help in the selection of materials and the creation of a visually appealing room. Not all are adept at kitchen design, so be sure to ask about one's expertise in this field.

▌ **General contractors** usually work from plans drawn up by another professional. They will get permits, install cabinets, and oversee the work of electricians and other tradespersons. Some specialize in kitchens and work in partnership with designers.

ABOVE Designed for a busy and sociable family, this room boasts efficient work space, places for guests to gather, a TV for the kids, and a wine cooler for the grownups.

LEFT The commercial-style range is meant for serious cooking. The island keeps household traffic out of the cook's way.

points of view

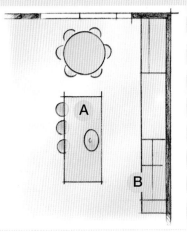

kitchen layouts

Available space and budget will dictate the size of your new kitchen. But you can establish an efficient layout no matter what the dimensions if you employ the work triangle—that is, place the range, refrigerator, and sink so they form the three points of a triangle and are no less than 4 and no more than 9 feet apart. Less space between the elements makes the work space too cramped; more space wastes steps, time, and energy. Traditionally, all of the layouts considered most efficient by kitchen experts were based on this work triangle. However, as kitchens have become multifunctional, new configurations may feature two or more work zones or activity centers. Choose the shape that best suits the space you have and the way you want to use it.

one-wall kitchens locate cabinets,

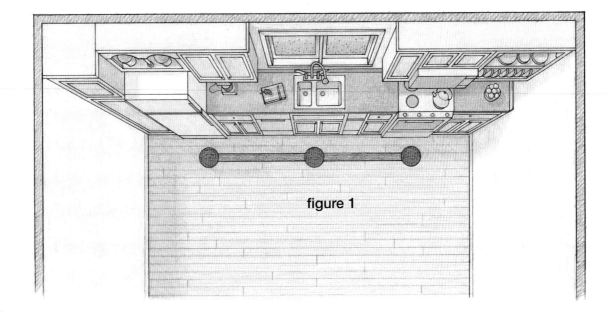

figure 1

counters, and appliances against a single wall ||||||||||||||

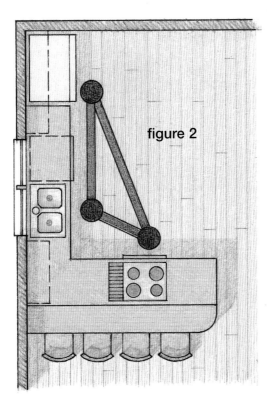

figure 2

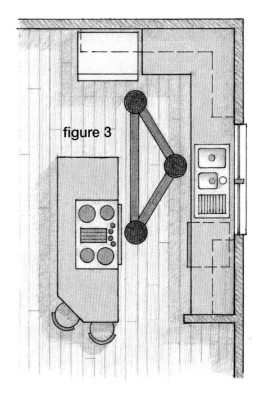

figure 3

OPPOSITE
Although most of this kitchen is arranged against one wall, a new clean-up center across from the snack bar improves the work space.

FIGURE 1 A typical one-wall arrangement.

FIGURE 2
Adding a peninsula or extending a line of cabinets creates a more efficient L.

FIGURE 3 If space permits, a cooktop can be located in an island.

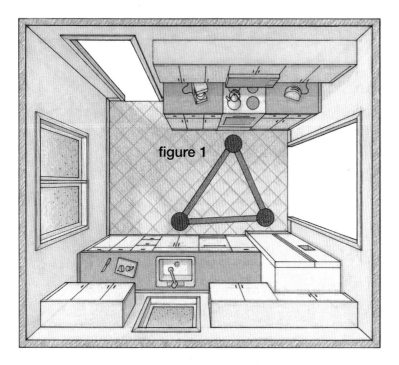

figure 1

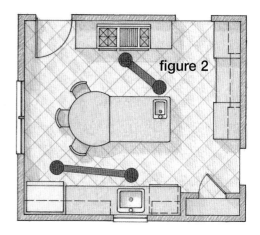

figure 2

how a galley kitchen works

RIGHT A galley kitchen places cabinets, counters, and appliances on opposite walls. Modest dimensions don't have to compromise efficiency when essentials are within easy reach of the cook.

FIGURE 1 A typical galley kitchen.

FIGURE 2 If space permits, create a secondary work zone or an eating area with an island.

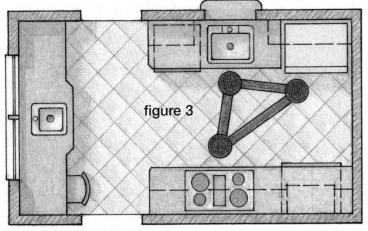

ABOVE Smart planning leaves space for a nearby eating area.

FIGURE 3 If possible, locate entryways outside the work zone.

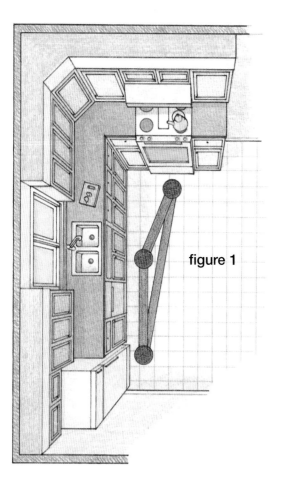

figure 1

||||||| an L-shaped layout offers more counter space |||||||

FIGURE 1 A typical L-shaped arrangement.

FIGURE 2 Installing a curved island diagonally across from an L configuration expands the possibilities of the work triangle.

figure 2

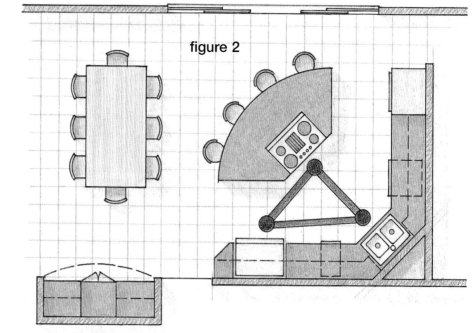

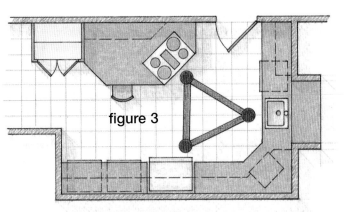

figure 3

FIGURE 3 By placing the range at an angle across from the L, the oven door, when open, will not interfere with traffic from the entry into the kitchen.

ABOVE In a large open plan, this L-shaped island forms a boundary that keeps company from straying into the work area.

RIGHT With the counters arranged along perpendicular walls, an L-shaped layout offers enough space for two people to work.

figure 1

ABOVE AND LEFT A hands-down favorite of design experts, a U-shaped kitchen boasts space for two cooks and multiple work triangles.

OPPOSITE TOP One section is devoted to wall ovens and extra storage.

FIGURE 1 A typical U-shape layout.

FIGURE 2 Large plans easily accommodate multiple work triangles.

FIGURE 3 A U-shaped eat-in kitchen.

U-shaped designs are highly functional

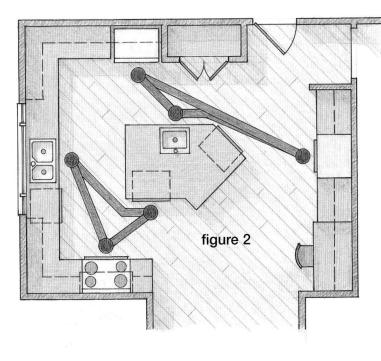

figure 2

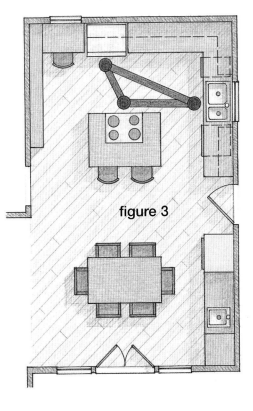

figure 3

a G-shape extends a U

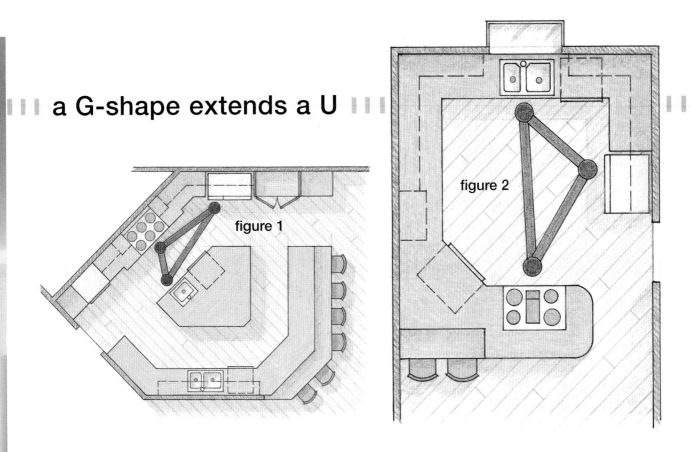

figure 1

figure 2

FIGURE 1 A large G-shaped layout allows two cooks to work together and has a generous amount of work surfaces.

FIGURE 2 The typical G configuration is a U with the addition of a short leg—usually a peninsula.

OPPOSITE This configuration permits placing the ovens in a separate zone away from the cooktop.

RIGHT Surrounded by the arms of the G, yet open to living areas around it, this self-contained kitchen ensures sociability.

islands and peninsulas

ABOVE A large granite-topped peninsula can elegantly seat four for lunch.

ABOVE An extra-large island provides a wide expanse for serving and dining.

ABOVE This island defines space, separating the kitchen from adjoining areas.

|||||| **define your**

ABOVE Even a small island can make an important difference. Here, an island added to an L-shaped layout provides counter area and storage.

bright idea

ample space

A countertop overhang of an extra foot can make maximum use of minimum space. Here, the cook can sit to read a recipe or sip a cup of tea.

work space and direct traffic away from it

Because no kitchen layout is absolutely perfect, consider beefing up yours with an island or peninsula. Islands improve function in several ways—they add counter space, hold a cooktop or sink, and provide storage or a surface for casual meals. Peninsulas perform similar functions and are often added to a U-shaped layout to produce a G. With cabinets accessible from both in and outside the work zone, peninsulas are a plus in busy kitchens.

LEFT A bi-level island has a tall counter for serving that hides a low surface.

RIGHT A hard-working butcher-block work table serves as an island.

OPPOSITE CENTER Two different styles, same smart use of a multi-functional design.

organize

RIGHT The two-level island in this elegant kitchen displays fine furniture details that blend with the traditional, white-painted cabinets.

OPPOSITE BOTTOM An apt addition to a farmhouse-style kitchen, this island resembles an old-fashioned pie safe.

bright idea

Casters

Do you yearn for an island that can move from one work station to another or roll into the dining room for serving? If so, look for one with casters on the legs. Thus equipped, the island will glide smoothly, then lock into place.

a rambling or inefficient layout and set the style

LEFT A wide aisle between the island and range gives two cooks room to work.

BOTTOM LEFT Build in conven-ience by attaching a desk at one end.

BOTTOM CENTER In an open-plan, hide the mess of cooking behind a tiled backsplash.

BOTTOM RIGHT An island cooktop will require vent-ing to whisk away smoke and odors.

OPPOSITE This island bake center was planned with a second sink and a dishwasher for efficiency.

extend work surfaces and storage

bright idea

pot racks

Hanging in artful disarray over an island, pots make a powerful design statement.

eat-in kitchens

H ere's a scenario that's especially popular these days—you lovingly prepare food, enjoying the company of family and friends while doing it, and then sit down to eat, all in the same room. There are many ways to make this warm and friendly fantasy a reality, even in a small kitchen.

If your new or remodeled design will be large, you can simply place a dining table somewhere in the room, taking care to position it at least a few steps away from the food-preparation area. In a modest-sized room you might build in a banquette or a booth along one wall or in an alcove. Space-saving banquettes are actually benches—usually upholstered for comfort—that lie along one or two walls in a corner and face a table. Space for a booth often can be carved out of the kitchen floor plan, too, although most booths don't seat more than four people. Islands and peninsulas can also provide space for snacks or quick meals but wouldn't be comfortable for diners who want to linger.

OPPOSITE TOP Clean-lined table and chairs for dining blend seamlessly with the contemporary look of the adjoining kitchen.

OPPOSITE BOTTOM A sunny spot under a window is a perfect location for space-saving banquette seating.

ABOVE An old wood table outside of the work center completes the farmhouse look of this spacious kitchen.

ABOVE RIGHT Think your kitchen's too small for a dining area? Look again. Maybe you can fit a table into a nearby corner. If it's a sunny corner like this one, so much the better.

RIGHT A wooden dining table and rattan-backed chairs add texture and warmth to this all-white eat-in kitchen.

bright idea

problem solver

A pullout table that is concealed behind a false drawer panel when it is not needed may be the answer when a full-size table is too large for a small kitchen.

ABOVE LEFT A mini table in a city kitchen provides ample space for dinner pour deux.

LEFT Thanks to careful planning, this compact kitchen has two eating areas—an island for breakfast and snacks and a table for dinner or parties.

OPPOSITE Placed near a door that leads to a terrace, this pretty kitchen table benefits from sunlight and views of the garden.

three **r**ules **f**or **e**at-in **k**itchens

▌ **Hide the mess** No matter how good the meal is, you don't want diners to have to look at the messy pots and pans that created it. If your dining table is near the work zone, shield cooking clutter with an island that's bar height—42 inches—on the table side and counter height—36 inches—on the kitchen side.

▌ **Keep the noise down** Eating in the kitchen is informal, yes, but don't let noisy appliances drown out all attempts at conversation. Dishwashers are the worst offenders. Invest in one of the super-quiet models, or make sure not to run the dishwasher at all until after dinner.

▌ **Lower the lights** Create a pleasant mood. "In my kitchen," says New York designer Rick Shaver, "the table is lit but I leave the undercabinet lights on in case I need something during the meal."

|||| add space for dining and create a heart-of-the-home ||||

Your eat-in kitchen will be anything but warm and friendly if you don't allow sufficient space for tables, chairs, and people. A rule of thumb—build in 12 to 15 square feet per person for comfortable and accessible dining. If you want to seat four adults, you'll need 48 square feet; to seat six, allow 72 square feet. Next, be sure there's enough space—about 36 inches is ideal—between the table and the wall so that people can sit, push their chairs back, and stand up. At the table itself, plan on 21 to 24 inches of space for each diner; a round table that measures 36 inches in diameter will seat four people; a 48-inch-diameter one will accommodate six. If you will use your island or peninsula for eating, remember the 21-inch-per person rule applies there, too.

OPPOSITE TOP An angle-shaped island visually relieves the rectilinear shape of this large kitchen.

OPPOSITE BOTTOM Mellow wood used in the kitchen and adjoining dining area gives this room an inviting ambiance.

RIGHT A glass dining table looks just right in this streamlined suburban kitchen.

BELOW This sociable design encourages guests to gather and chat with the cook before sitting down to dinner.

Y ou've made a couple of important decisions—to remodel your kitchen and to make it good looking and inviting. But exactly what kind of look do you want? One that is traditional, country, or contemporary? The style that's right for you will probably harmonize with the design of your house inside and out. If the architecture is classical, a formal traditional look may be right. Country styles seem to suit people who enjoy a casual and relaxed lifestyle. A contemporary design will be a good choice if you like clean lines and a minimum of accessorizing.

Select a Style

I traditional I country I
I contemporary I

Bold color and sleek lines are hallmarks of this contemporary Retro Modern kitchen. Patches of eccentric green with a few turquoise accents add a one-of-a-kind look.

When you have chosen the look you love for your kitchen, you will find that the cabinets set the stage. In traditional kitchens, where the ambiance is elegant, gracious, and just a little bit formal, cabinets are most commonly crafted of rich, gleaming woods, usually cherry or mahogany or any wood stained to resemble them. Ivory- or white-painted cabinets are another frequent choice, but the key to the cabinets is a rich, glossy finish and the look of fine furniture. For the cabinet door style, choose a raised-panel design and

traditional

such architectural details as crown moldings and other millwork. Countertops, which are typically made of a glossy, polished stone such as granite or marble—or a solid-surfacing or plastic laminate look-alike—may also feature rich details such as bullnose or beveled edges. Choosing countertop colors of deep green, dark gray, or black will add richness, as will wood floors or a classic black-and-white checkerboard pattern in ceramic tile or vinyl. One of the reasons for the popularity of this gracious style is its timelessness and the fact that it is unaffected by design trends that come and go.

LEFT Featuring formality on the light side, this kitchen in the American traditional style combines light wood, granite counters in a pale shade, and lots of sunlight. The chandelier strikes the right formal note.

OPPOSITE BOTTOM LEFT To maintain the traditional look, the front of the side-by-side refrigerator/ freezer is disguised by full overlay panels that are custom-made to match the cabinetry.

BELOW LEFT Curved-back chairs and a china cabinet with fine-furniture detailing grace the eating area. Muntins on the patio doors are a nice touch.

RIGHT This design relies on a crisp black-and-white tiled backsplash and honey-toned cabinets for its all-American appeal.

bright idea

Coffee station

This little corner is reserved for an espresso machine. The granite countertop is stylish and practical as a heat-resistant surface.

southern accents

ABOVE A generous island welcomes family and friends to gather in front of the cooking hearth.

LEFT Drawers and cupboards in a wide variety of sizes answer every possible storage need.

BELOW This room mixes plain Southern pine cabinets with fancy details: crown molding, turned legs, and roped and fluted pilasters.

bright idea

distinct design

Crown moldings and other millwork are key to the gracious look of traditional kitchens.

french flavor

ABOVE Formal cabinetry with handsome detailing and brass hardware defines this traditional kitchen. The focal point is a bay window that frames views of a pretty garden. A hammered-copper front on the exposed-apron sink adds French-style texture.

LEFT A mélange of elements contributes to the French traditional look here—white-painted cabinetry, colorful tiles, rattan dining stools, and copper accents throughout.

a take on tuscany

TOP Natural materials and earthy colors reveal the Tuscan inspiration for this design.

ABOVE LEFT An unfitted look is also essential to the style. Here, sturdy farmhouse-like cabinets and furniture are deliberately mismatched, then done up in different colors.

ABOVE RIGHT The dining area glows with color and texture—a wood ceiling, tile floor, olive-color walls, and deep-red chairs. A wrought-iron chandelier tops it off beautifully.

RIGHT The cabinets are slightly distressed for an appropriately rustic look.

OPPOSITE FAR RIGHT Arches and other classical motifs enhance the Old World atmosphere of the room. A huge island provides supplemental storage.

timeless customs

What could be more European than a thick and frothy cappuccino? And what could be more appropriate in an Old World-inspired kitchen than a coffee station? The one pictured here has been created inside a bank of cabinets with slide-in doors. But aside from an espresso machine, what other elements go into creating what we call Old World style? The look is actually a mix of French and Italian with a little Greek and Roman classicism thrown into it, too. Nothing should look shiny or new. The overall effect is comfortable with obvious signs of wear and tear. Richness in color, material, and texture is also key—rugged limestone or tumbled marble; ceramic tile; mellow woods; and disparate elements that seem to have been lovingly added piece by piece over time.

Some kitchen designers and other experts in the field theorize that we love the country look because it recalls the warmth of Grandma's kitchen, conjures up romantic notions of the keeping rooms of old, or simply links us to what we believe was a simpler, gentler time. Whatever the reason, this is an extremely popular style, and opportunity for personal expression abounds. Informal and relaxed, country is a good choice for a casual lifestyle; and because the look of wear and tear is desirable, it suits busy families and active kitchens, too. Build your country kitchen around wood cabinets in a natural stain, a pickled or bleached finish, or a cheerful paint color. Neither elegance nor sleekness is the goal; so mismatched cabinets, freestanding unfitted pieces, or open shelves filled with dishes are also appropriate. Wood floors are ideal but homey patterns in vinyl or tile would also work. Almost anything goes for countertops, but especially something that's earthy —a rustic stone or tile, for example.

country

There are many offshoots of this basic look—English country, cottage, Victorian, and Arts and Crafts, to name a few. If you're the country-kitchen type, one of these variations is sure to please you. Shown here is another variation on the theme, the new look of American country, a slightly more sophisticated style with sleeker lines and fewer accessories than its predecessor.

RIGHT This design takes country to a sophisticated new level. Cabinets with sleeker lines and elegant granite counters intermingle here with the usual down-home charm and informal mix of woods and hardware.

TOP In keeping with the heart-of-the-home country philosophy, the kitchen is open to an inviting family dining area.

ABOVE Even a sleek version of country allows for personal expression. Cookbooks, family photos, and framed prints occupy a corner of the room.

RIGHT An interior window opens into an enclosed porch and is used as a pass-through for informal meals.

country style has many

OPPOSITE TOP For those who love log cabins and the outdoor life, this style is a great choice for the kitchen. The warm tones of the wood cabinets make it cozy, and the arched window frames a woodsy view. Note the distinctive Arts and Crafts details on the window and hanging lamp.

OPPOSITE BOTTOM LEFT A massive fieldstone arch encloses the cooking center and creates the aura of a hunting lodge in the woods.

OPPOSITE BOTTOM RIGHT In addition to providing a work surface and extra storage, the sturdy, rustic island is an important decorative element. Wood flooring is a comfortable choice for underfoot.

LEFT Extensive use of mellow wood is the key to this cabin-style kitchen. The butcher-block island holds a handy second sink that allows two people to work on food preparation together.

creating the cottage style

An amalgam of English country and Victorian bungalow, the cottage kitchen ranges from rustic to refined. An all-white scheme puts the room shown here in the refined category, but all the key elements of the overall style are represented—painted wood cabinets, beadboard backsplash, plate racks, and glass-fronted cabinets. Other versions of a cottage kitchen might include colorful, mismatched, and slightly worn-looking cabinets and vintage furniture and accessories.

looks, from rustic cabin to cozy cottage

LEFT Simple cabinets with a hand-made appearance and exposed beams and rafters contribute to the rural air of this farmhouse kitchen.

BELOW LEFT Period-style faucets resemble the pumps that once brought water to kitchen sinks. These days they're handy for filling tall pots.

BELOW RIGHT Essential to the look is a kitchen table where people gather. The island serves this purpose and doubles as a food-preparation counter.

american farmhouse versus

a lived-in look

The English country style does not derive from the great houses of the English countryside but from modest homes and bungalows that have been lived in comfortably for generations and are pleasantly cluttered. To re-create this style, choose cabinets with a patina of age and details such as plate racks, niches, glass fronts. For floors, wood or matte-finish tile works well; countertops may be stone, solid-surfacing, or wood—any material that does not look shiny and new. The desired effect resembles an Old World kitchen, but the colors are lighter, and personal collections of English china are key.

english country

ABOVE Intricately designed cabinets are a sure sign of English country, as is the warm cream paint color that looks gently aged.

RIGHT Much of this kitchen's charm comes from vintage linens and china that seem to have been collected over many years.

RIGHT Old World-style offers an interesting alternative to American country, featuring earthier colors, a stronger emphasis on stone, cabinetry that resembles unfitted pieces of antique furniture, and mellow patinas.

BELOW An alcove with a rustic-looking wooden bench and tall casement windows is an inspired Old World touch.

old world style

bright idea
the niche
A built-in shelf within the cooking hearth can be decorative or useful as a place to keep infused oils or spices handy.

OPPOSITE Details make the difference—a large arched window, Italian mosaic tiles on the backsplash, and the matte finished faucets and hardware all suggest another time and place.

RIGHT Wide aisles between the center island and the work zones make this warm family kitchen comfortable no matter how crowded it gets.

ABOVE Au courant appliances and fixtures complement the kitchen's decor.

LEFT Style-wise, there's a little bit of everything from classical columns to a kitschy collection of vintage cookie jars. Mixed with a sure hand, all of the elements are harmonious.

anything goes

An eclectic kitchen is very personal. It brings together elements from different styles and eras and makes them visually cohesive. It's not easy to pull off, but this advice from designer Rick Shaver of Shaver-Melahn in New York City should help. "There must be a common thread, be it color, texture, architectural detail, even collectibles," says Shaver, who designs furniture as well as interiors. The kitchen shown here relies on architectural detail to unite its disparate elements. Another eclectic design might be held together thematically by displays of collections such as bowls, kitchen utensils, or transferware.

eclectic style mixes it up

ABOVE An imposing bank of black-painted upper cabinets is a surprising touch that works because it looks like an old china cabinet.

ABOVE RIGHT A backsplash of windows brightens the look by day; cabinet lighting takes over at night.

RIGHT Details from several styles and eras—including a mid-century kitchen set—enliven the room with a unique point of view.

ABOVE This updated contemporary-style kitchen is definitely streamlined, but not sterile. The warmth of the cabinets' wood stain, the gentle curves of the two-level island, and the rounded backs of the dining chairs soften its appearance.

LEFT True to the contemporary philosophy, the sleek cabinets are without embellishment, except for the curvilinear brushed-steel hardware and occasional glass-panel door.

OPPOSITE Countertops in natural materials, such as the granite used here, are a hallmark of contemporary kitchens. Countertop edge treatments are typically plain—either squared off or bullnosed and without bevels.

The contemporary style had its origins at the end of the nineteenth century when artists, architects, and designers rebelled against the fussy and cluttered design sensibility that prevailed throughout most of the Victorian era. Their rebellion manifested in simplicity and the use of natural materials. As the look evolved it continued to emphasize natural materials but became more and more streamlined. For a time, in the 1970s and '80s, when newly emerging technology was impacting the culture, a "high-tech" look was de rigueur in many kitchens. These designs were sleek and hard-edged; articulated in the neutral tones of stainless steel, stone, and glass; and looked almost like laboratories. Although contemporary style remains pared-down for the most part, it has warmed up considerably since then.

contemporary

The backbone of today's contemporary kitchen is frameless, flat-panel cabinetry with clean lines and simple hardware. Wood finishes, particularly maple, cherry, and birch in lighter tones, are common choices. Cabinet doors made of glass and metal—often aluminum—are popular, also, because they go well with sleek contemporary appliances. Natural surfacing materials—especially stone, tile, and concrete—or solid-surface laminate versions dominate surfaces. The Retro Modern, or Mid-Century Modern, look that can be seen in home furnishings is also influencing kitchen design. Sleek and industrial in a 1950s-70s way, it may not be for everyone, but it has a growing following.

retro modern

ABOVE Touches of the 1950s, such as curved-back plastic chairs and expanses of chartreuse, qualify this design for the retro-chic category.

LEFT A retro-style mixer in turquoise, a favorite '50s color, is an apt accessory.

RIGHT The wild color on the walls, countertop, and tile collage along the backsplash are in stark contrast to the spare contemporary cabinets and the subdued brushed metal finishes.

revisiting the recent past

A decorating style that revisits mid twentieth-century designs, Retro Modern is a manifestation of the contemporary genre. The retro chic philosophy does not suggest that you entirely re-create the look of the era; you can incorporate just a few telling details. For example, to retro-fit your kitchen with a '50s flavor, you might add diner details, such as chrome stools topped with red-leather seats or plastic-laminate countertops with the reissued boomerang pattern. Retro-style appliances are available from several manufacturers, too.

If you are fond of contemporary interiors but afraid that a kitchen designed in this clean-lined, unembellished style is doomed to look cold and clinical, think again. The contemporary kitchen has evolved over the last few decades, and the "high-tech" laboratory look is out, replaced by a warmer, friendlier version. Today's contemporary-style kitchens are still simple, spare, and equipped with the latest technology, but a new focus on wood for the cabinets and the restrained use of color as an accessory makes them as appealing and inviting as any traditional or country-style kitchen. Study the rooms on these two pages to see the influence of wood and other softening elements in state-of-the-art yet personal spaces.

warming trends

RIGHT Backsplash tiles in an earthy red-orange have a powerful warming effect in this room. Curvy chairs soften the cabinets' hard edges.

BELOW Cooktop venting equipment, which is typically encased in stainless steel, is covered in wood that matches the cabinets.

TOP In an interesting juxtaposition of styles, a clean-lined kitchen opens into a dining space with an ornate chandelier and eighteenth century-style chairs.

ABOVE Prominent grain running through the wood provides visual appeal. It also keeps the stained blue-gray cabinets from looking stark, especially next to the stainless-steel hood.

glass act

Frosted-, opaque-, textured-, wavy-, or etched-glass cabinet doors hide a multitude of sins. Behind them, cabinet contents look interesting but don't have to be neat as a pin. In addition, they don't show fingerprints as easily as clear-glass panels.

classic white

LEFT Crisp lines, polished granite countertops, and expanses of white cabinetry give this room its classic character. The mirrored back-splashes, angled island, and arched window inject visual liveliness.

TOP RIGHT In another classic-white kitchen, a stone backsplash and countertops reinforce the sleekness while adding texture. A countertop appliance provides the right dash of color required to ease the starkness.

RIGHT In this small city kitchen, light is an important factor in making the space seem larger than it is. Windows are left uncurtained in keeping with the style and to flood the room with sunlight.

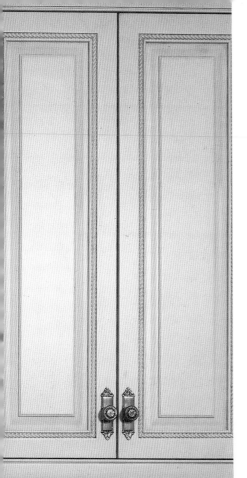

Cabinets, often called the backbone of the kitchen, will represent a major part of your construction budget. The number of cabinets you choose and their arrangement will establish the basic layout of the room, and perform the important task of organizing and storing all of the accoutrements of food preparation. Other elements of kitchen design—appliances, countertops, and wall and floor finishes—flesh out the basic structure established by the cabinets. Get your money's worth by shopping and buying smart. In this chapter you'll find information to help you make the best choice for your needs.

Cabinet Choices

I design anchor I cabinet construction I
I manufacturing styles I
I measuring for cabinets I

Choose kitchen cabinets carefully. They should be strong, durable, and attractive, while also offering enough storage to contain all of your cooking essentials.

ABOVE LEFT A "cabinet" for the range hood reinforces the country theme.

ABOVE Simple white cabinets set the stage for a country kitchen.

LEFT A mini butler's pantry stores china, linens, and flatware.

design anchor

Cabinets perform two important functions in the kitchen—they store and organize the necessities for cooking and they determine the design of the room. Other factors, such as countertop and flooring materials, appliances, wall and window treatments, and accessories, contribute to appearance. But cabinets are the most visible element and are therefore most responsible for the overall look.

In the kitchens of the last century, furniture was used haphazardly to hold dishes, pots and pans, and utensils, but they didn't necessarily match each other or anything else in the room. That mismatched, "unfitted" sort of look is popular again today with some homeowners, but most people prefer cabinets cut from the same design cloth to provide a unified look for the kitchen.

Once you have chosen the layout that meets your needs and the design style that reflects your taste and personality, you're ready to go cabinet shopping. Take your time. Whatever style you have settled on will be available from every major manufacturer of kitchen cabinets. Visit showrooms, look at calalogs, log on to company Web sites, and study the choices within the category you prefer. Get cost estimates, too. Armed with cost information and a rough idea of how many cabinets you'll need, you'll have a ballpark budget for the cabinet portion of your new kitchen, which according to experts, is about 40 percent of the total.

A foolproof way to figure how many storage cabinets you'll need is to empty the contents of your present ones and combine everything you want to store. Each pile of dishes, pots and pans, flatware, table linens, and cookbooks will represent one, or maybe more, of the cupboards and drawers you now require. If this method proves too disruptive and time-consuming, study your present storage situation and estimate how much more you will need, allowing for items that you'll accumulate over time.

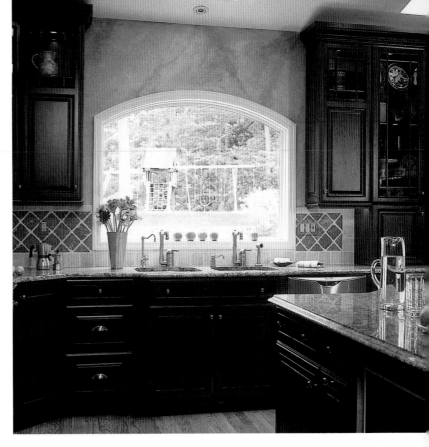

ABOVE In this design, richly embellished cabinets furnish the flair.

BELOW Fine-furniture detailing enhances the elegant ambiance.

RIGHT Dark stain and fancy trim distinguish this china cabinet.

BELOW Unique handles are appealing.

LEFT Stately cabinets with a honey-toned stain and recessed panels make a strong design statement here.

BELOW In this space, white-painted, recessed-panel cabinets are responsible for a crisp country look. A tall corner unit topped by crown molding maximizes the farmhouse-kitchen flavor.

bright idea

details that deliver

Want to heighten visual drama in your kitchen? Add unexpected touches such as ornate architectural details, a chandelier in the work zone, or formal draperies.

ABOVE Looking for glamour in the kitchen? Choose dark, rich-looking cabinets with ornate trim; then add such touches as a chandelier, draperies, and a gilt mirror.

LEFT Panels of bird's-eye maple heighten the glamour, as does the crystal-like hardware.

cabinet construction

Thousands of manufacturers produce attractive cabinets in a huge variety of styles, finishes, and prices. But not all of them are well-built. Before you buy cabinets, scrutinize their construction details. Beware of drawers that are nailed, glued, or just stapled together. Well-made drawers should support about 75 pounds when open. Cabinet cases should measure at least ½ inch thick all around, and interiors, including rear surfaces, should be finished. Adjustable shelves are another sign of quality. Make sure they measure at least ⅝ inch thick to prevent bowing. Look for solid hinges that don't squeak and allow doors to open fully. Some fine cabinets are made of solid wood, but a plywood box with solid-wood doors and frames also offers good structural support. Less pricey but acceptable units mix plywood supports with medium-density fiberboard doors and drawer fronts, or feature a laminate finish over high-quality, thick particleboard. Stay away from drawers made of thin particleboard.

cabinet door style choices

Door styles are strictly decorative. Styles pictured, left to right: reveal-overlay panel; frame and panel; flat panel; beaded frame and panel; square raised panel; curved raised panel; beadboard panel; and cathedral panel

OPPOSITE LEFT This cabinet sports two sure signs of high quality and careful construction—finished interiors, including the back panel, and strong hinges.

OPPOSITE RIGHT A specialized cabinet keeps spice jars handy to the cooktop. Sturdy shelves, finished to match the surrounding units, have a convenient wipe-clean surface, a feature to look for when cabinet shopping.

LEFT A mellow finish, precise design detail, and handsome brass hardware contribute to the traditional look of these kitchen cabinets.

ABOVE A recent kitchen innovation, refrigerated drawers place often-used foods in close proximity to work counters. Another convenience—the interior lights up when you open the drawer.

options

As you shop for cabinets, think about building specialized areas where family and friends can come together—a home office, a place for kids to do crafts or homework, a bar, a baking zone, even an entertainment center. Inquire about cabinet options that incorporate convenient features.

RIGHT This clean-up center includes china and glassware storage, saving you trips across the room to put things away.

BELOW Positioned close to the work zone in the same kitchen, a compact home office boasts plenty of drawers, a roomy desktop, and shelves for books and collectibles.

TOP In a busy family kitchen, a microwave occupies one end of the island, out of the cook's way.

ABOVE Details such as this ornate bracket contribute a touch of elegance to the room.

LEFT Multi-purpose cabinetry includes a bar area and a niche for a TV.

ABOVE Carve out a corner in a busy kitchen for a planning desk. This one features a desktop, cabinets, and pigeonholes for organizing papers.

BELOW Conveniently situated steps away from the back door, a potting area with a porthole window would delight any gardener.

RIGHT Making the most of a few feet of wall area, this planning desk shares space with a wine cooler.

BELOW LEFT Treated with a lighter finish and door style than the rest of the cabinetry, an angled display cupboard filled with collectibles commands attention.

BELOW RIGHT A variation on a classical fluted column embellishes this corner.

framed vs. frameless construction

In framed construction, a rectangular frame outlines the cabinet box to add strength and provide a place to attach the door. The doors on frameless cabinets are laid flush over the box. No frame is visible, and hinges are often invisible as well.

▌Frameless A European concept that took hold here in the 1960s, frameless cabinets are a standby in contemporary kitchens. The doors fit over the entire cabinet box for a sleek and streamlined look.

▌Framed Cabinets with a visible frame offer richness of detail that is appropriate for traditional and country kitchens and their many design cousins.

ABOVE Standard-sized units in this semi-custom design are laid out in an arrangement that suits the needs of the homeowners.

RIGHT Another way to create an individual look—use the same basic cabinet style but vary finishes.

There are several ways to buy cabinets for your new kitchen. *Knock-down (KD)* units go home with you the same day, and if you can install them without hiring a professional, the price is right for a tight budget. Mass-produced *stock* cabinets, issued only in standard sizes and in limited styles and finishes, are also an economical choice if quality is good. *Semi-custom* cabinets are restricted to standard sizes too, but the variety of styles, finishes, interior options, and accessories is much greater, expanding design options considerably. *Custom* cabinets, available from some cabinet companies or from local cabinetmakers, are built to your exact specifications and measurements. You'll pay a premium price, but you'll get a one-of-a kind kitchen with a personalized look and endless storage possibilities.

manufacturing styles

ABOVE This curved island was custom-created, like the rest of the cabinetry, for this high-end kitchen.

ABOVE RIGHT Other made-to-order touches to consider include glass-fronted units in a variety of sizes and specially outfitted interiors.

RIGHT This custom-made cabinetry strikes the right note in the kitchen of a late nineteenth century house.

LEFT Framed cabinet doors in a natural stain create a country look.

RIGHT AND BELOW RIGHT Architectural trim, inlays, and other fine-furniture details can make cabinets look especially elegant.

OPPOSITE A custom finish imparts the look of an aged cupboard.

frame a cooking area with cabinetry

These two custom-designed cooking zones are distinguished by range-hood enclosures that match surrounding cabinets, blend seamlessly with the overall design, and create appealing focal points.

bright idea
stock up on style

For visual appeal and
a custom look in a kitchen
fitted with stock cabinets,
mix in a few glass-panel
units and vary the sizes,
heights, and even finishes
of the other units.

look high and low—you'll discover unexpected places to

ABOVE Smart cabinet systems make the most of available space. Here, every inch of wall area is put to efficient use.

LEFT Otherwise-wasted space between ovens and a planning desk has become a useful bookcase; the TV pulls out and swivels.

RIGHT High cabinets hold serving dishes, keep placemats tidy, and stow vases behind glass doors.

beef up storage

ABOVE LEFT AND RIGHT Creative use of a skinny space between ovens and the wall—a pull-out unit just wide enough for a broom and dust pan.

ABOVE LEFT AND RIGHT Making maximum use of mere inches on either side of a cooktop cabinet, a slide-out unit is added for spice jars, and a tall slot for baking sheets.

corners

Wasted corners are the enemy of convenience in the kitchen. But the cabinets shown here have conquered corners and transformed them into useful storage areas such as pantries for canned and packaged foods, ABOVE LEFT AND RIGHT, deep drawers devoted to pots and pans and their lids, LEFT, and an especially clever angled cupboard for bottles, RIGHT.

the right height

According to kitchen planners and designers, the most accessible storage compartments are positioned roughly between eye level and knee height. Organize your storage so that often-used items fall into this range; then stash items that you rarely use above and below these points.

nooks
and crannies

Small but important storage areas can put wasted space to work. A lighted niche, for example, is set into a backsplash in a cooking alcove, ABOVE LEFT. Recessed into a wall near another cooking area, a shallow cabinet ensures that spices are handy, LEFT. (A pot-filler faucet is a helpful addition.) Carved out of a narrow space between cabinets, another nifty niche holds dishtowels, ABOVE.

OPPOSITE TOP LEFT A two-tiered drawer encourages tidiness.

OPPOSITE TOP RIGHT Divisions in this drawer prevent cooking utensils from ending up in a jumble.

OPPOSITE MIDDLE LEFT Cleaning products, usually stowed under the sink, are more accessible in a deep drawer.

bright idea

storage savvy

Standard cabinets are not the most efficient places to store pots, pans, and their elusive lids. Special tall pull-out cabinets do the job, too. Deep drawers are also great— the pots lift out easily; and as the drawer slides out, you can see its entire contents.

OPPOSITE MIDDLE RIGHT A pot rack provides both easy-to-reach storage and an interesting focal point.

OPPOSITE BOTTOM LEFT A divided drawer tames odds and ends.

OPPOSITE BOTTOM RIGHT In this two-tiered unit, pots occupy a deep drawer while a shallow drawer keeps lids in line.

RIGHT A multipurpose unit keeps wine at the right temperature and offers luxuriously roomy storage for pots, pans, and the accompanying lids.

LEFT Transparent bins are a colorful and convenient way to store pasta and dried beans.

RIGHT A slide-out spice rack utilizes a dead zone between the range and a base cabinet.

plan your storage and create a clutter-free kitchen

LEFT This pantry cabinet includes a couple of easy-access bins for canned goods.

RIGHT A clever cupboard is built into otherwise unused space at the end of an island.

BOTTOM LEFT A message center features a phone, answering machine, pull-out writing surface, and drawer for pads and pencils.

BOTTOM RIGHT When pulled out, this drawer becomes a landing under a microwave.

OPPOSITE As this kitchen illustrates, today's cabinets come in enough sizes and shapes to meet any home-owner's needs.

the shape of things

STANDARD CABINET DIMENSIONS (in inches; ranges in 3-in. increments)

Cabinet	Width	Height	Depth
Base unit	9–48	34½	24
Drawer base	15–21	34½	24
Sink base	30, 36, 48	34½	24
Blind corner base	24 (not usable)	34½	24
Corner base	36–48	34½	24
Corner carousel	33, 36, 39 (diameter)	X	X
Drop-in range base	30, 36	12–15	24
Wall unit	9–48	12–18, 24, 30	12, 13
Tall cabinet (oven, pantry, broom)	18–36	84, 90, 96	12–24

RIGHT AND OPPOSITE TOP The cabinet system in this kitchen includes an island that doubles as a bake center.

OPPOSITE BOTTOM LEFT A built-in coffee station is a favorite feature.

OPPOSITE BOTTOM RIGHT This easy-access pantry cabinet has handsome louver-style doors.

typical dimensions

Alter these typical dimensions to suit your needs. For example, many people prefer a 37½-inch counter height, and tall people are more comfortable working at an even higher counter.

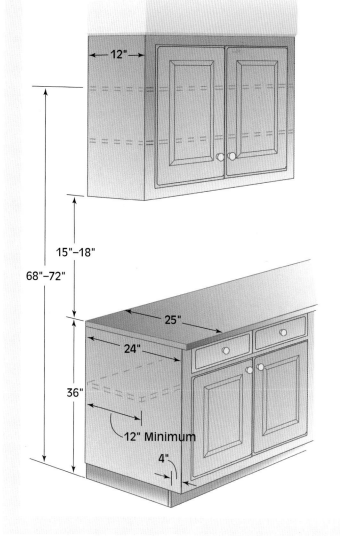

measuring

Start planning by making a rough floor plan of your kitchen, noting doors, windows, and other breaks in the walls. Measure at three heights—above baseboards, at 36 inches, and at 6 or 7 feet. On paper, start assembling the cabinets and appliances you require. Don't worry if they don't fit exactly. Cabinet widths progress in increments of 3 inches, and by juggling sizes, you can usually put together a series of units, making up the differences with filler strips. Corners can be tricky. Ask your designer or contractor about specialty units like blind bases or corner bases. Or consider adding a corner sink or a peninsula to make use of corner space.

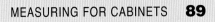

for cabinets

TOP LEFT An efficient baking center features slots and slide-out baskets that organize everything necessary for making the perfect pastry.

TOP RIGHT A recycling station with four bins makes sorting easy.

MIDDLE LEFT Drawer-like baskets under a food-preparation counter are ideal for storing fruit and vegetables close to the point of use.

MIDDLE RIGHT This unit pulls out to dispose of recyclables or trash; close it, and clutter disappears.

BOTTOM LEFT Substituting frosted-glass panels for clear ones subtly heightens design appeal.

BOTTOM CENTER With their hint of antiquity, leaded-glass doors would be a nice touch in a traditional or English country kitchen.

BOTTOM RIGHT Ribbed and textured glass has great impact in this contemporary kitchen.

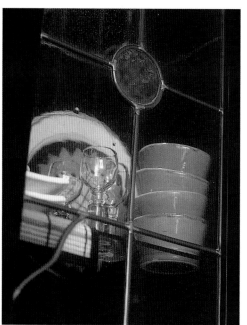

get a handle on it

Cabinet hardware is such an important element these days that some designers call it "the jewelry of the kitchen." As the four examples below illustrate, you can find hardware to suit any style of kitchen, from ornate to graceful to old-fashioned to streamlined.

Although cabinets will be the most recognizable element in your kitchen, the surfaces—walls, floor, and ceiling—that surround them will also impact the look of the room. Selecting materials and finishes wisely can make the difference between a visual hodge-podge and a harmonious design. But it's not all about looks. There are practical considerations, too. If the surfaces you select are easy to maintain and able to withstand daily wear, you'll spend less time cleaning and more time enjoying your new kitchen.

Surfaces

❚ wall treatments ❚ flooring ❚
❚ ceilings ❚

Warm painted surfaces enliven this kitchen and pull together such disparate elements as the stainless-steel appliances and a dark-stained maple floor.

While you're focused on cabinets, appliances, and countertops for your new kitchen, don't let the walls get lost in the shuffle. The way you finish the walls will define your style and pull the design together.

Paint is the easiest and most economical wall treatment, unless you choose a decorative finish that requires a specialist. And if you want to trim the budget a little, you can do the painting yourself. Whatever color paint you decide to use, select a washable finish. And remember—ceilings don't have to be white. Painting them a lighter version of the wall color or a very pale blue is more interesting.

Wallcoverings, such as a washable vinyl, cost a little more than paint but are still quite economical to apply, especially if you do it yourself with prepasted and pretrimmed rolls: a variety of colors, patterns, and coordinating borders are available, with new ones introduced yearly.

wall treatments

Paneling, another smart surfacing choice, is the most effective way to cover up imperfections in an existing wall. The word "paneling" refers to planks or sheets used as a wall surface, and it doesn't have to look like the dreary knotty-pine you may remember from "finished" basements of the past. In fact, some paneling is quite elegant and expensive. There is a middle ground, however, with a variety of woods or wood look-alikes that can add warmth and character to your kitchen. Wainscoting, which is paneling that goes to chair-rail height, is a popular choice for country-style kitchens.

OPPOSITE A brick-red wallcovering with a subtle design enriches other warm tones in the kitchen and blends with the colors in the adjoining room, too.

ABOVE Zesty green paint looks refreshing above a half wall of white ceramic tiles.

LEFT Treated to resemble plaster, these creamy-white walls complement the elegant cabinetry and materials in this room.

▮ how to create a rusticated stone wall

1 Draw a grid for the blocks; then apply painter's masking tape to create mortar lines. Vertical lines should be staggered and centered. Pounce on paint, twisting the brush to create a stonelike texture. Vary the coloration by applying different amounts of pressure with the brush.

2 Allow the blocks to dry, and pull off the tape. With a darker shade of paint, create shadow lines along the right or the left and the bottom of the blocks. Use an artist's brush and a broad knife as a guide. To make the shading subtle, first thin the paint with a little water.

3 When the shading lines are dry, thin full-bodied white paint, and paint the mortar lines around the blocks. Leave the shadow lines untouched except for slightly clipping their bottom corners. The final "stone wall" is now complete with an overall mottled appearance with highlights and shadows.

OPPOSITE AND BELOW   A "stone" wall created with faux-painting techniques accentuates the European farmhouse flavor in this kitchen.

RIGHT   A glazed finish in an open-plan kitchen and family room softens the geometric window arrangement.

BELOW RIGHT   A ragged and glazed paint finish makes these walls look well worn and interesting. Their color blends beautifully with the fabrics and furniture in the room.

try a faux finish on the wall

wallpaper and **p**aint

When it comes to kitchen wall treatments, there is only one hard-and-fast rule—use washable paints and cleanable, nonporous wallcoverings. Here are a few other decorating tips:

▌ Bold, deep paint colors will warm up the kitchen; cool colors create calm; prints and patterns add liveliness and cheer.
▌ Not sure that a particular color or pattern will work? Apply paint or a large wallcovering swatch to a piece of poster board; hang it on the wall; and see how you like it as the day changes. Still love it? Live with it for a week before making a decision.
▌ To establish harmony throughout your house, choose a wall treatment that's in sync with the rooms that adjoin the kitchen.

OPPOSITE TOP LEFT Washable wallpaper in a simple medium-scale print unifies this kitchen and adjoining sitting room.
▌
OPPOSITE TOP RIGHT A rich saturated green is an effective backdrop for a contemporary kitchen.
▌
OPPOSITE BOTTOM Crisp and cool, this kitchen mixes bright blue wall paint with a white ceiling, cabinets, and trim.
▌
LEFT The bold use of color—such as this terra-cotta tone—can transform a room from ordinary to warm and vibrant.
▌
BELOW Neutral but rich, the buttery off-white paint on these walls aptly accompanies the Arts & Crafts-style cabinets.

popular trimwork profiles

Greek and Roman details are a part of so many decorating styles that it's hard to find ornamental trim without some kind of classical design. The ogee shape, for instance, appears on everything from interior trimwork to exterior cornices to table edges. Here are some of the basic molding shapes and motifs that have withstood the test of time.

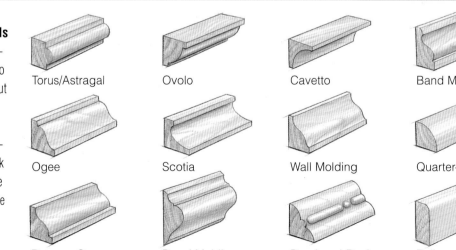

Torus/Astragal

Ovolo

Cavetto

Band Molding

Ogee

Scotia

Wall Molding

Quarter-Round

Reverse Ogee

Panel Molding

Bead-and-Reel

Bullnose

trimwork

Architectural trim— a category that includes door and window casings, moldings, baseboards, and columns—is the crowning glory of a well-planned room, like a ribbon that puts the final beautifying touches on a gift package. It's important that you choose ornamentation that matches the style and proportions of your kitchen and the architecture of your house. Choices vary from simple to elaborate, as the drawings here illustrate. Ornate detailing works well in traditional rooms; simpler trim is more suitable for casual or contemporary settings. If you're after a really fancy effect, you may have to enlist a cabinet-maker, but check your lumber-yard or home center for precut or ready-made possibilities.

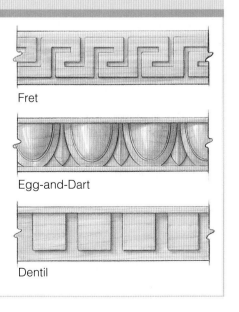

Fret

Egg-and-Dart

Dentil

OPPOSITE AND ABOVE White window and door trim, baseboards, and crown molding stand out against tomato-red wall-covering to create depth and distinction.

RIGHT Fluted columns give the passageway into this traditional kitchen a sense of importance.

classic columns

Ionic Column with Entablatures

Cornice

Frieze — | Entablature

Architrave

Capital

Corinthian Capital

Shaft

Doric Capital

Base

ABOVE LEFT AND RIGHT Whether they are original or reproductions, bull's-eye corner blocks and dentil-molding trim can add big design impact to a kitchen window.

LEFT Mitered casing distinguishes this door frame.

the difference between dull and distinctive is in

Pilaster Construction

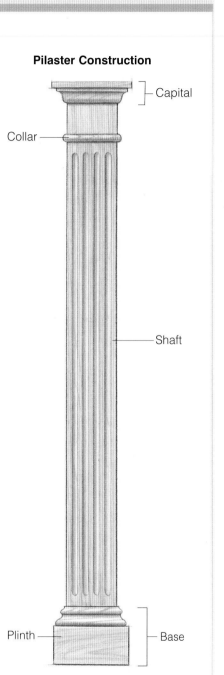

Capital

Collar

Shaft

Plinth — Base

RIGHT The focal point of this food-preparation area is a Federal-style, round-top window richly decorated with trimwork to match the cabinet trim and crown molding.

the details

door and window casings

VICTORIAN-STYLE MITERED CASING

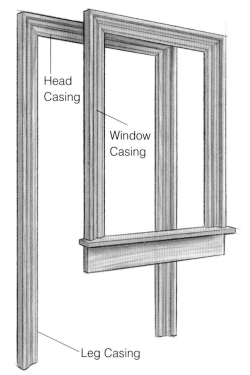

Head Casing

Window Casing

Leg Casing

BELLYBAND CASING WITH ROSETTE

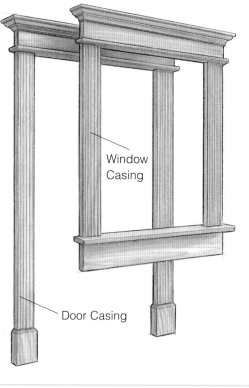

Window Casing

Leg Casing

ARTS AND CRAFTS–STYLE CASING

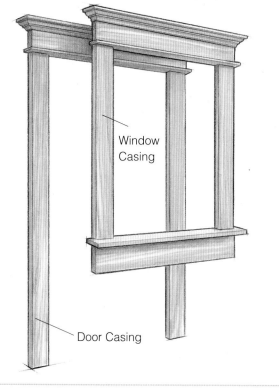

Window Casing

Door Casing

FLUTED CASINGS WITH DECORATIVE HEAD

Window Casing

Door Casing

OPPOSITE TOP
Low-profile clamshell moldings accentuate the otherwise undressed windows and glass doors in this contemporary room.

OPPOSITE BOTTOM LEFT AND RIGHT
Create design distinction the quick and easy way by applying wallcovering above beadboard wainscoting. Add more interest with coordinating wallcovering borders and simple chair-rail and picture-rail moldings.

bright idea

paint power

In a clean-lined room, make no-frills clamshell trim pop out pleasingly by painting it a color that contrasts with the walls.

LEFT Sheet vinyl flooring is available in many patterns, including this brick look-alike.

OPPOSITE TOP LEFT A wood floor is a natural choice for a simply stated, New England-style country kitchen.

OPPOSITE TOP RIGHT A ceramic-tile floor with diamond-shaped insets echo the pattern in the backsplash of a classic black and white kitchen.

BELOW Linoleum, a popular material from 1900 to the 1950s, is back with updated patterns and colors.

Most of the flooring materials on the market today combine good looks with low maintenance and durability, all of which are important qualities for use in the kitchen. Because looks are important in this highly visible room, you'll want a floor that blends with the cabinets and other elements that you have chosen. When you go shopping, keep design harmony and appropriateness in mind. Wood works well with virtually any kitchen style, but stone, suitable for a contemporary room, may not be right for some traditional kitchens, and a minimalist material, such as concrete, must be used judiciously. Also, ask questions about the cleanability of the materials you like. No flooring is completely maintenance free, of course, but some require less attention than others. How much cleaning are you willing to do? The answer to this question will help you choose. Here's another important question: how much comfort do you want underfoot? Some materials—wood, vinyl, and laminate, for instance—"give" better than others. If you'll be on your feet for long periods of time preparing complicated recipes for large numbers of people, you may want to go for a material's cushioning effect and forgo something less-forgiving, such as ceramic tile and stone. Learn about degrees of durability, too. Most modern materials are designed to stand up well to wear and tear, but if your kitchen is an especially high-traffic area, with kids and pets running through it, you'll need something that's especially tough. Select the highest quality and most durable product that you can afford and avoid "bargain" materials that you will have to replace in a few years.

flooring

▮ how to refinish a wood floor

1 Load a medium-grit belt on the sander, and sand in the direction of the wood strips. Keep the tool moving to avoid damaging the floor.

2 After two passes with the sanders, vacuum completely and apply either a stain or the first coat of polyurethane.

3 Allow the polyurethane to dry, and then buff with a steel-wool disk attached to a rotary buffer. Follow the grain of the wood when buffing.

4 Make sure the floor is completely clean (you may want to run a tack cloth over it), and apply at least one more coat of finish.

BELOW The pronounced grain in this natural cherry floor provides a slightly informal look that suits the relaxed elegance of the kitchen.
▮
OPPOSITE TOP Oak, laid on the diagonal to break up the small space, is a perennial flooring favorite.
▮
OPPOSITE BOTTOM Light-toned Canadian maple works well in both traditional and contemporary settings.

wood

Wood floors introduce warmth and a feeling of comfort to the kitchen, but some types work better than others in this busy room. Oak, maple, ash, and other hardwoods stand up better than softer pine, fir, or cherry to the pounding a kitchen floor takes. A wood floor finished on-site with oil or wax has a beautiful sheen, but it will need yearly refinishing. A polyurethane finish lasts longer and requires no stripping, waxing, or buffing. High-quality prefinished flooring, an increasingly popular alternative, eliminates the time, mess, and toxic fumes of the floor-finishing process. There is also increasing interest in hand-scraped wood, which is hand-distressed for a rustic appearance. It looks old, but its finish is up to date and durable. Properly finished wood floors are easy to maintain, and minor spills are not a problem. However, continued exposure to water, around the sink or dishwasher for example, could cause warping or buckling.

ceramic tile and stone

Ceramic tile and stone are popular kitchen flooring materials, and no wonder. Ceramic tile is durable, moisture proof, easy to maintain, and available in such an enormous range of colors, sizes, and shapes that its design potential is practically infinite. Tiles that mimic stone are particularly popular right now. So are the stone materials themselves, especially granite, slate, limestone, and soapstone, all of which also offer durability and easy maintenance, but they must be sealed. Ceramic-tile costs range from moderate to pricey; stone is generally more expensive. If you choose any of these materials, put safety first and select textured, matte finishes that provide slip resistance. The down side? Ceramic tiles and some types of stone can crack if something heavy falls on them—whatever falls will likely break, too. Other possible drawbacks: these materials are noisy when you walk on them, and they are cold and hard underfoot. What's new and trendy? Tinted, painted, and stained concrete.

LEFT A border of tan-and-white mosaic tiles enlivens this ceramic-tile floor; the tiny tiles decorate the backsplash, too.

ABOVE Two unique ceramic-tile patterns coexist peacefully in this open kitchen-dining area.

RIGHT A floor of soft-beige ceramic tiles flows smoothly from kitchen to dining area, establishing design unity between the two spaces.

bright idea

accent

Define a part of your kitchen—such as this dining spot— with a "rug" composed of tiles.

basic tile shapes and patterns

The basic floor tile measures 12 x 12 in. with ⅛- to ¼ -in. grout joints.

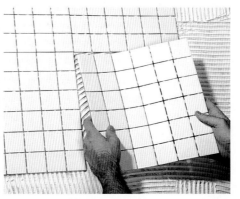

Sheet-mounted tile will look like individual mosaic tiles when installed.

Rectangular tiles can create basket-weave patterns.

Combining different shapes allows you to create a variety of patterns.

Hexagon-shaped tiles create an interlocked pattern.

Multicolor and **multisize tiles** are available in sheets.

LEFT A colorful arrangement of ceramic squares and tiny mosaic tiles acts as a border between the cabinets and a slate floor in this kitchen.

RIGHT AND BELOW For a country-style kitchen, the owners chose a wood floor for the food-preparation area because of its casual good looks and ease underfoot. In the adjoining dining area, the flooring changes to unglazed terracotta tiles interlaid with wood strips that unite the two areas aesthetically.

vinyl and linoleum

Resilient vinyl flooring has been hugely popular since the 1960s. Low-cost, low-maintenance, and durable, it is available in a multitude of colors and looks. In addition, it has a certain amount of built-in cushioning, making it comfortable while you stand and work. It's smart to invest in a high-quality product with a tough wear layer and a generous amount of cushioning. Every vinyl floor will show wear eventually, but a medium-toned background with a definite pattern will look good longer than a light or white background with very little pattern. Vinyl comes in sheets or tiles.

Linoleum, which lost favor because it required waxing and sealing, is now available presealed, so it's easy to maintain. It is pricier than vinyl, but durable, comfortable underfoot, and available in a modest array of colors and patterns in sheets or tiles.

OPPOSITE TOP AND LEFT Some resilient sheet vinyl flooring, such as these parquet and plank patterns, resembles wood.

RIGHT This black-and-white flooring, with the crispness of ceramic tile, is actually resilient sheet vinyl.

BELOW LEFT With this scored and speckled sheet vinyl, you get the look of stone at a fraction of the cost.

BELOW A contemporary design of vinyl floor tiles enhances this sleek kitchen.

the next best thing to wood and stone

laminate and engineered wood

Laminate flooring can look like stone, tile, or other materials, but it is best known for its realistic mimicry of wood strips or planks. The visible layer of this multilayer product is a photographic image, which is then covered with a tough melamine coating. Bonded together under high pressure, the layers add up to an extremely durable floor that under normal circumstances can handle heavy kitchen traffic and withstand such mishaps as scratches, burns, and stains. Walking or standing on a laminate floor is comfortable, and it's easy to maintain and economical, although somewhat more expensive than vinyl. Most laminate floors "float," which means they are not nailed or glued to an underlayment, and they can be installed over most other materials, including wood, concrete, vinyl flooring, or ceramic tiles. There are a number of laminate-flooring brands, and quality varies. To get the best product for your needs, ask about thickness, durability, and the life expectancy of the flooring. Because a damaged laminate floor cannot be recoated or repaired, it's important to look into warranties as well.

Engineered wood, like laminate, consists of several layers—typically three to seven—that are bonded together under heat and pressure. The top layer, a hardwood veneer, is available in almost any wood species. As a result of the layered construction, manufacturers claim that engineered wood is less susceptible than solid wood to damage from moisture or changes in humidity. More expensive than laminate, but less than solid-wood products, engineered wood can be installed over a variety of subfloors.

LEFT A laminate floor patterned after stone introduces warmth and texture to this country-style kitchen without breaking the remodeling budget.

OPPOSITE FAR LEFT This scored laminate looks like rugged stone but is softer and more comfortable underfoot.

LEFT Hard to distinguish from the wood it imitates, a faux-maple laminate floor stands up to the traffic in a busy family kitchen.

RIGHT Laminate flooring is available in a variety of wood patterns. This light-toned pecan look-alike is a good choice for a contemporary-style kitchen.

The ceiling? Just paint it white—nobody notices it. If that is your attitude, you're missing a wonderful opportunity to introduce detail and warmth to your kitchen—and to inexpensively eliminate existing flaws while you're at it.

Even a simple coat of paint on the ceiling can make a difference. A light, neutral, or pastel shade of paint will be more interesting than white and will increase the feeling of light and spaciousness in the room. A medium or dark hue will create coziness and intimacy.

Ceiling tiles and panels take things a bit farther by adding texture of various kinds and becoming part of the room's design. There are many types available—some with a subtle

ceilings

textured look; others with more definite, decorative patterns. Metal tiles that re-create the look of pressed-tin ceilings common in turn-of-the-last-century rooms are also available in a variety of sizes, patterns, and finishes, including tin, copper, and brass. They are sure to make a big impact when added to a country or period-style kitchen. Your lumberyard stocks sections of tongue-and-groove and beadboard planks that resemble porch ceilings of the past, another way to bring the charm of the past to a kitchen of the present. Before you embark on a ceiling treatment, be sure that it's in keeping with the feel of your house in general and with the style of your kitchen in particular.

LEFT Wood beams, newly installed to create rustic charm, look like they've always been there.

OPPOSITE TOP New 2-ft.-square suspended plaster tiles supply instant architectural detail.

OPPOSITE BOTTOM LEFT The look of an old pressed-tin ceiling tops off this traditional kitchen.

OPPOSITE BOTTOM RIGHT Wood planks are reminiscent of the porch ceilings in older houses.

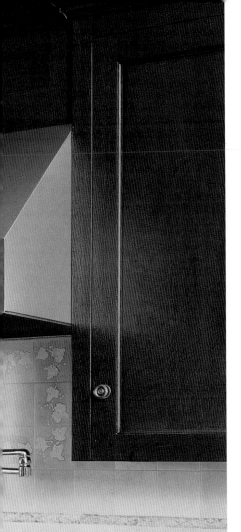

The kitchen is the heart of the home, and appliances are the heart of the kitchen. But hold on to your hat—these days there are enough choices to make you dizzy. The first thing you'll notice is a new look. Many appliances are so sophisticated and beautifully designed that they almost qualify as furniture. Another trend—convenience. You can customize equipment to suit your cooking style, mix and match fuels, order features that think for you, and save energy at the same time. Before you shop, arm yourself with a ballpark budget and a clear understanding of your needs.

Major Appliances

| cooking | ventilation |
| refrigeration | dishwashers |
| laundry |

Everybody loves professional-style ranges. This model is 36-in. wide, has four cooking elements and a large oven, and fits easily into a modest-sized work area.

Although most families are busier than ever, they still love home cooking. And the manufacturers of today's cooking appliances are making it easy to prepare fresh meals in short order. Some new ranges and ovens roast or bake foods in a fraction of conventional cooking times. And a suit-yourself approach allows you to customize these appliances according to your cooking style, using either gas or electric, or a combination of the two. The influence of professional equipment, still going strong after more than a decade, can be seen

cooking

in both the look of conventional ranges, ovens, and cooktops, and in their performance, particularly the ability to control heat precisely. For example, commercial-style hi-lo burners can stir-fry at a searing 15,000 Btus or melt chocolate at a simmering 500 Btus. (Btu stands for British thermal unit, the measurement for heat output.) A dual-fuel range combines gas burners with an electric oven, and a separate cooktop can feature both gas and electric cooking elements. For two-cook kitchens, minicooking stations, called "hubs," can be configured as you wish, with one or two burners plus a steamer, a grill, or a deep fryer, for example. Warming drawers are hot again, a convenience for families on different schedules and for entertaining. In the midst of this speed and convenience, quality is paramount. Buy the best you can afford, even if you have to sacrifice special features.

OPPOSITE LEFT TOP A commercial-style range has what serious cooks want—two ovens and six burners that can deliver precise heat levels.

OPPOSITE LEFT BOTTOM An eclectic kitchen combines a new vintage-look range and state-of-the-art wall ovens.

OPPOSITE Well-equipped for all kinds of cooking and entertaining, this room includes a cooktop, two wall ovens, a microwave, and a powerful range hood.

ranges

Ranges come in several styles. With unfinished sides, *slide-in* (below) and *drop-in* (bottom) ranges are least costly. Slide-in models fit between two cabinets; drop-in models are installed on a base matching the cabinets. *Freestanding ranges* have finished sides and can stand alone.

ABOVE A restored 1930s stove appeals to nostalgia lovers. BELOW LEFT The "Refrigerated Range" keeps food cool all day until programmed to start cooking. BELOW RIGHT A two-oven range prepares multiple dishes at different temperatures.

OPPOSITE TOP For this small kitchen, the homeowner chose a streamlined ceramic-top cooktop and built-in, full-size oven that doesn't protrude into the work aisle.

OPPOSITE BOTTOM RIGHT The cook who designed this kitchen combined a five-burner gas cooktop, a favorite with gourmet chefs, with a built-in oven that has a sleek contemporary look.

ABOVE Sealed burners are an easy-to-clean convenience as well as a safety feature. They prevent spills from leaking into the burner box.

RIGHT This pro-style gas cooktop boasts six continuous cast-iron grates that create a larger cooking surface. This design lets you move heavy or large pots to another area on the cooktop by sliding rather than lifting them.

types of cooktops

Gas cooktops, top, start up fast, cook evenly, and are easy to control. Coil-style **electric** cooktops heat up quickly but cool slowly; they cost less than gas cooktops but can be more costly to operate. Also electric, **ceramic-glass** cooktops, bottom, heat up very fast; their sleek glass surface is easy to clean. **Halogen** and **induction** types both have glass surfaces and both cook by heating the cookware, not the cooktop. Like gas, induction cooktops offer quick response and precise control, but cost more and require specific types of cookware.

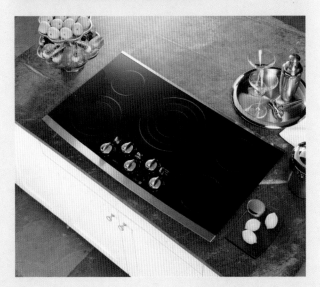

bright idea

hi-lo burners

With this nifty innovation, you can simmer your favorite chocolate sauce.

LEFT A customized compact cooktop may combine a two-burner, ceramic-glass unit with a steamer, for example.

ABOVE For meat-and-potatoes meals, combine a deep fryer and a grill.

OPPOSITE This dual-fuel cooking station features a high-output gas burner, a steamer, and an electric cooktop.

customizing a **c**ooktop

These days, selecting cooking options is as creative an endeavor as cooking itself. The concept of hubs, fresh from Europe, has made possible minicooking centers that may contain a gas burner and an electric element, plus a grill, griddle, or any combination of them. Larger cooktops can also receive this individualized treatment. The result—you can put together a cooktop that precisely suits your needs and install a second separate cooking station for another cook or smaller meals.

ABOVE This stainless-steel microwave and convection oven bakes, browns, roasts, or grills foods up to five times faster than a conventional oven.

LEFT A full-extension oven rack lets you baste or turn foods without taking them out of the hot oven.

RIGHT Stacked ovens save space and steps. Defrost food in the microwave, roast it in the oven, and then keep it on hold in the warming drawer.

OPPOSITE A custom wood-fired oven gives a unique taste to roasts, pizza, vegetables, and more.

RIGHT AND FAR RIGHT This kitchen has got it all. The versatile electric warming drawer keeps cooked foods hot or encourages dough to rise. The cooking zone contains a restaurant-style gas cooktop, a microwave, and two wall ovens.

ovens

Conventional gas and electric ovens cook via heated air; pricier electric convection models add one or more fans for faster, more even cooking and browning. Steam ovens cook food quickly and, some say, more healthfully. Microwaves, the least costly option, cook very fast but don't brown foods. In a big hurry? The new speed ovens, which combine convection and microwave technologies, reportedly cook eight times faster than other methods. Even faster—and more expensive—are ovens that mainly use light (high-intensity halogen bulbs) to cook foods. They'll roast or bake foods in a quarter of the time required by conventional ovens. But unless the recipe you are preparing has been programmed into the oven's computer chip, you'll have to experiment at first to get the cooking time right.

sizing ventilation fans

No matter how attractive the hood may be, it is the fan in the system that actually takes the air out of the kitchen. Fans are sized by the amount of air they can move in cubic feet per minute (CFM). Here are some guidelines to help you size the ventilation fan to suit your needs: multiply the recommended CFM below by the linear feet of cooking surface. Note: the length of the ductwork, the number of turns in the duct, and the location of the fan's motor also contribute to the size of the fan needed.

RANGES AND COOKTOPS
installed against a wall:
Light Cooking: 40 CFM
Medium to Heavy Cooking: 100 to 150 CFM

RANGES AND COOKTOPS
installed in islands and peninsulas:
Light Cooking: 50 CFM
Medium to Heavy Cooking: 150 to 300 CFM

ABOVE A wood-clad range hood with traditional styling whisks fumes away from an island cooktop.

LEFT A sleek chimney-style hood can be used with a cooktop or a range.

RIGHT This metal hood and backsplash boast a custom-finished patina.

ventilation

Ventilation systems are perhaps not as sexy as top-of-the line cooking equipment, but without one your kitchen will smell like a down-at-the-heels diner in no time. A hooded ventilation system, installed directly over the cooking surface, is the most effective way to expel smoke, grease, and nasty odors. The hood captures cooking air as it rises, and a fan expels it outside through a duct. Place your range hood so that it overlaps the cooking surface by 3 inches on each side and sits from 24 to 30 inches above it.

Hoodless downdraft ventilation, used with island cooktops, forces the air above the burners through a filter, then out of the house via ductwork. It's not as effective as a hooded system but better than a ductless fan, which can't do a good job.

ABOVE Restaurant ranges require large hoods and powerful ventilating systems.

ABOVE RIGHT A straight-sided pro-style hood complements this cooktop.

RIGHT Downdraft venting is an alternative system.

LEFT A brick tile wall and custom range hood give this cooking center a cozy look.

BELOW LEFT A paneled exhaust hood coordinates with the walls, and the metal backsplash adds plenty of pizzazz to the cooking area.

BELOW A plaster-covered hood and the tile mural below it add Old World flavor.

OPPOSITE TOP LEFT AND RIGHT European-inspired hearth-like cooking centers have become increasingly popular, as these custom-designed alcoves illustrate.

the range hood's role in the new home hearth

BELOW LEFT AND RIGHT Examples of the redesigned "hearth" include a mantel-style range-hood cover and a clock. Both incorporate fine architectural details.

ABOVE Create a built-in look with a 24-in.-deep, side-by-side refrigerator that's flush with the cabinets; then add custom-made panels that match the cabinetry.

ABOVE RIGHT In this brushed stainless-steel combination model, the freezer is on top and features an in-the-door filtered-water and ice dispenser.

LEFT This trendy new French-door unit offers a tilt-out freezer drawer that makes it easy to access frozen items. Double doors open to the fresh-foods section.

efrigerators and freezers have come a long way. Current models have sleek good looks and smart features we could barely have imagined a decade ago. And all of them consume less energy. The most important advance, however, is the ability to customize these appliances and their features to suit your cooking, cooling, and entertaining needs.

As always, you have a choice between a separate refrigerator and freezer and the more common combination of the two within one model. Combination models include refrigerator and freezer side by side, freezer on top, or freezer on bottom configurations. Side-by-sides keep both fresh and frozen foods easily accessible, but only the largest sizes can efficiently store the bulkiest items. With bottom-mounts, fresh foods are at eye level, but freezer access requires bending; top-mounts do the reverse, so your choice may depend on which section you need to access most. Nowadays you can rethink this large, central cooling appliance in favor of modular or smaller under-counter refrigerators or freezers placed at various zones in the kitchen according to need.

cooling

There's big news inside the new cooling equipment, too. Storage is more flexible and customizable. There is room in some models for platters of party food, two-liter soda or wine bottles, bulky frozen foods, and other items you used to have to jam in to fit. "Elevator" shelves slide up smoothly, and glide-out shelves make it easy to find items that can get hidden in the back. Some models have two thermostats or dual compressors so that humidity levels in fresh-food and freezer compartments can be controlled separately; that way, lettuce won't wilt in order to keep ice cream frozen, for example. Another plus—there is no transfer of odors from one compartment to another. Inside the fresh-foods compartment, there may be several temperature zones so that you can store fruits and vegetables differently from meats, dairy products, or beverages. Express features on some refrigerators chill certain foods super-fast or cut thawing time in half. Cooling equipment is now designer equipment too, especially at the high end. Some stainless-steel units have the commercial look that many people love; retro, 1950s-style units with up-to-date interiors come in bright colors that really stand out. If you're not going to call attention to your chic refrigerator you can follow another significant trend by integrating it with the look of your kitchen. Select a built-in or 24-inch-deep unit that fits flush with the cabinets or hides behind cabinet doors.

LEFT In a traditional-style kitchen, overlay panels make the bottom-mount, built-in refrigerator look like one of the cabinets.

RIGHT Blending appliances with cabinets is one way to approach kitchen design. But as this kitchen illustrates, stainless-steel appliances do not necessarily detract from the woodsy warmth and graciousness of a country-style design.

custom **r**efrigeration

In the old days, the refrigerator ruled. We put the bulky combination unit in a central place, if possible, then clustered our work zones around it to save steps. These days, thanks to the flexibility of modular cooling units that can be placed anywhere in the kitchen, we are no longer slaves to that one immovable behemoth, which is a special blessing for multiple-cook kitchens. We can provide point-of-use convenience in the bar area with a compact under-counter unit and an ice maker, or supply a secondary cooking station with a drawer-style refrigerator or freezer. Many combinations are possible—so get creative and customize.

classy cover-ups for cooling equipment ⏐⏐⏐⏐⏐⏐⏐⏐⏐⏐⏐⏐⏐⏐⏐⏐⏐⏐⏐

OPPOSITE FAR LEFT Looking like a handsome piece of furniture, this customized built-in design is clad in wood overlays that match the cabinets. The top section holds fresh foods; the top drawer contains beverages; and the bottom drawer is a freezer and ice maker.

ABOVE LEFT AND RIGHT In the closed position, these drawers look like part of the cabinetry, but they open to reveal a small refrigerator with a freezer and ice maker below it—a perfect combo for a bar area or beverage center.

LEFT To reduce the bulky look of the large 48-in.-wide refrigerator their family needed, the homeowners covered it with elegant wood paneling that blends with the cabinets.

RIGHT See-through glass doors, an idea borrowed from the pros, are handy if you're willing to keep refrigerator contents neat and tidy.

bright idea

ice maker

Never run out of ice with a separate ice maker. A compact, under-counter model can be fully integrated with your kitchen cabinets.

ABOVE LEFT AND RIGHT Refrigerators that measure only 24 in. deep fit flush with surrounding cabinets (see the side view) for a streamlined, built-in look.

LEFT A wine cooler built into the island is easily accessible during parties, yet out of the cook's way.

RIGHT Under-counter cooling is an especially hot kitchen trend, with modules designed for specific functions and point-of use convenience. Here, an icemaker complements a three-shelf beverage refrigerator.

BELOW Don't let the retro styling and 1950s colors fool you—these refrigerators are strictly up-to-date with such features as 20.9 cubic feet of interior space, spill-proof glass shelves, and spacious door storage.

dishwashers

Using a dishwasher will save you about four hours of labor a week, according to the Association of Home Appliance Manufacturers. As you shop for this important labor-saving device, you'll find some significant improvements in energy efficiency and noise levels. Some new models use fewer than 5 gallons of water for a standard cycle; others heat the water faster. In some of the fancier units, sensors detect the amount of soil on the dishes and automatically select the proper temperature and number of cycles. With this feature, you'll no longer need to run the appliance on an energy-wasting maximum setting for every use.

Dishwashers are also reportedly 50 percent quieter these days, provided you choose a well-insulated model. A simpler noise-control option—select a delay-start feature and run the machine after you've gone to bed. Energy costs may be lower then, too. Dishwashers measure 18- or 24-inches wide. Large families or those that frequently entertain will need the bigger model and maybe a second one. For consistently small loads, an 18-inch unit or a compact dishwasher drawer may be sufficient. Consider these other features and options: stemware racks; split baskets for small loads; zone cleaning; strong, normal, and soft water jets; extra-large capacities; and dual drawers. Make your choice based on the way you cook and clean; when you shop, take along any tall or awkward items that you wash regularly to be sure they fit in the dishwasher before you buy it.

OPPOSITE TOP LEFT Ideal for a contemporary-style kitchen, this dishwasher offers a curved stainless-steel front and a touch-pad control panel.

OPPOSITE TOP RIGHT A second dishwasher was built into the island, across from the sink.

OPPOSITE BOTTOM A three-tier interior has a bottom rack for pots and pans and large utensils.

ABOVE AND ABOVE RIGHT In these kitchens, overlay panels dress up the front of the dishwashers to match surrounding cabinets.

RIGHT With the touch-pad controls located inside the door rather than on the front of the unit, this dishwasher can be completely camouflaged by a custom cabinet-drawer panel.

near-the-sink **a**ppliances

Used near—or in—the sink in conjunction with dishwashers, garbage disposal units and trash compactors are handy supplements that make cleanup speedier and life easier.

▌ **Garbage disposal units** are those handy devices that grind up organic wastes and flush them down the drain in the kitchen sink. Continuous-feed disposals keep working as long as cold water is running and peelings, paring, and leftovers are being fed into them. Controlled by a switch on a nearby wall or cabinet, the continuous-feed disposer is the least expensive option. Batch-feed unit disposers can grind up 1 to 2 quarts of waste at one time. They are controlled by a built-in switch that you activate by replacing the strainer on the drain. Batch-feed models are safer to use—and more expensive. Before you install either of the units, check local building codes.

▌ **Trash compactors,** which measure from 12- to 15-in. wide, are available as freestanding or under-counter models and are typically placed near the main sink or a secondary one. Trim kits are available to make this appliance blend with other cabinetry. They compress inorganic waste, such as cans, bottles, paper, plastic, and dry food waste to about a quarter of their original size, thus greatly reducing the amount of inorganic garbage and trash you have to handle. If you pay by the bag for garbage removal, a trash compactor may be a wise investment. Some models offer a key-activated safety feature, toe-touch latch, and automatic deodorizer.

OPPOSITE TOP A smart idea for a busy kitchen, this secondary food-preparation area is equipped with a small sink and a small-capacity dishwasher drawer.

ABOVE LEFT Trimmed to match cabinets, dual dish drawers operate independently for energy-efficient small loads and wash delicate items separate from pots and pans.

LEFT In a beverage center, a convenient dishwasher in a drawer takes care of glasses and coffee cups at the point of use.

ABOVE With dual drawers, or two full-size models, you'll never have to unload the dishwasher.

the

ABOVE Freestanding or built into a kitchen cabinet, a "personal valet" is an at-home dry-cleaning system.

BELOW LEFT AND CENTER Side-by-side or stackable front-loading units are good choices for a kitchen laundry center.

BELOW RIGHT Match cabinetry when the laundry room is visible from the kitchen.

You spend a lot of time in the kitchen, so why not do the laundry there, too? It makes a lot of sense—and it sure beats trudging up and down the basement steps for every load of wash. In a kitchen with generous dimensions, you'll probably have space for a washer and dryer (48 to 58 inches wide for full-sized, side-by-side machines), but it's

laundry area

important that you locate them outside of the main food-preparation area so that they not impede traffic flow when in use. Allocate space, too, for laundry supplies. Front-loading models with a control panel on the front can be tucked under the countertop, thus blending them into the room and creating counter space for folding clothes or supplementing kitchen work space. Another good idea—select stackable units and build a cabinet to enclose them. Top-loaders will also fit into a good-sized kitchen, but because they can't be slid under a counter, they are more likely to become eyesores, unless you can conceal them behind folding or pocket pantry doors that don't open into the work aisle. Also, consider a built-in ironing station that can be installed inside a cabinet.

BELOW A laundry room that's adjacent to a kitchen has matching countertop and flooring materials.

There have been many changes since the last time you went shopping for a kitchen sink. The old standbys, porcelain and stainless steel, are still available, but there are more options to consider—bigger sizes, deeper bowls, new configurations, and colors and materials galore. Faucets, too, offer more finishes and features than ever before. In spite of their increasing allure, sinks and faucets are still the workhorses of the kitchen, so it's important that the choices you make look good and work hard.

Sinks and Faucets

▌ sinks ▌ faucets ▌

Kitchen cleanup's a breeze with a pair of stainless-steel sinks. The stylish high-arc faucets come with helpful extras, such as a spray attachment and a soap dispenser.

Here's a helpful rule of thumb for choosing a kitchen sink—identify your practical needs first, then go for good looks. With so many choices you won't have to sacrifice one for the other. Another pointer comes from the National Kitchen & Bath Association (NKBA), an industry trade group: a standard 22 x 24-inch single-bowl sink is sufficient for kitchens that measure 150 square feet or less; for kitchens that are over that size, a larger single-bowl design or a double- or triple-bowl model are better choices.

If you haven't bought a kitchen sink for a while you'll be dazzled by your choices. And you may be surprised that many kitchens, even relatively modest ones, sport two or even three sinks. There's the primary one, located at the heart of the work area near the dishwasher and devoted to cleanup. There may also be a small prep sink, often located away from the busiest area and intended for a second cook or for a helpful dinner guest who may be washing or chopping vegetables or fruit. This secondary sink, a nice amenity for any household, is practically a necessity for a two-cook kitchen. If you have a large family or entertain often, you may want to install a bar sink that allows people to help themselves to beverages without getting in the cooks' way. If this auxiliary sink is accompanied by an undercounter refrigerator and enough counter space for a coffeemaker, you've got a beverage center.

Unless you select unusual shapes, super sizes, or deluxe materials such as natural stone, concrete, copper, brass, fire clay, or handmade ceramics, kitchen sinks are not especially big-ticket items. An investment of

a couple of hundred dollars will get you a high-quality single- or double-bowl model in porcelain, stainless steel, or a composite material. The price could go up several hundred more for color, multiple bowls, or solid surfacing, and you'll pay another premium for apron-front farmhouse sinks no matter what the material.

OPPOSITE TOP AND BOTTOM
In this busy kitchen, the farmhouse-style main sink is divided. One side is for rinsing dishes that are destined for the adjoining dishwasher, the other for washing platters or soaking pots. A smaller sink that is used for food preparation and drink-making is located a few feet away in the island.

RIGHT AND BELOW RIGHT In another multiple-sink kitchen plan, the primary sink sits in the work island, and a bar sink occupies a spot on the other side of the room. Unusual high-arc faucets add practicality and panache.

BELOW A deep farmhouse-style sink with an exposed apron front is a good choice for this airy, country kitchen. Across a generous aisle, safely out of range of the busy food-preparation area, a smaller auxiliary sink is available for use by a second cook working at the island.

popular **m**aterials

When it's time to choose a kitchen sink, you can go for the glamour, selecting a material such as stone, hand-painted china, or even glass. But if you want to make a more conventional choice, there are some solid options for your consideration.

The familiar look of glossy white porcelain over cast iron has great appeal for many people, and this durable material is also available in myriad colors. Stains that may develop over time are generally easy to remove. A perfect match for trendy pro-style appliances, **stainless steel** is affordable, easy-care, and long lasting; 18- or 20-gauge steel promises durability and strength, and a satin finish disguises most water spots and scratches. Other metals, such as **copper** and **brass,** look great but require lots of care and polishing. Used alone or molded into a countertop, **solid surfacing** comes in many colors and stone-looks. It's pricey but requires little maintenance; the occasional scratch, dent, or stain can be successfully repaired. Often used for trendy farmhouse sinks, **concrete** and **soapstone** are costly but practically indestructible. Soapstone comes in several earthy colors, and concrete can be tinted any shade you like.

OPPOSITE In keeping with the sensibility of an Old World kitchen, the exposed apron sink is made from hammered copper.

ABOVE LEFT AND CENTER LEFT Two-bowl sinks are handy for busy kitchens. Here, one is clad in stainless steel; the other is fashioned from solid-surfacing material.

ABOVE Doing dishes is fun in a lively hand-painted sink made of durable, nonporous fire clay.

BELOW LEFT The off-center drain in this deep-bowl porcelain sink increases usable space.

BELOW This handsome sink is formed from trendy concrete.

LEFT Because the color goes all the way through, granite composite sinks don't fade over time. This brilliant blue is one of several lively shades available in the material.

ABOVE Offering the look of 100-percent real stone without the big price tag, this white quartz-composite sink boasts two bowls; the small one is ideal for rinsing fruits and vegetables.

LEFT BOTTOM This granite-composite sink is extra long, making it handy for washing large items such as pots and platters; an off-center drain makes the job even easier.

OPPOSITE Versatile composite sinks can be mounted under or dropped into a kitchen counter. This drop-in model is formed from granite composite, which is available in black, as shown, and in white, ivory, gray, and other stone-like shades.

3 main composite materials

Ever since plastic laminate was cooked up in a laboratory early in the last century, product engineers have been working to create materials that supply the look and durability of stone but cost less. One case in point: composites, which are available in three basic types.

Polyester/acrylic is the least expensive and least durable of the big three. It's somewhat soft, so it scratches and stains easily. Still, if your budget is tight, you'll like its price, glossy surface, and bright colors.

Quartz composite, a mixture of crushed quartz and resin fillers, is durable and resistant to most stains and scratches. Its moderate price and earthy or bright colors, including a brilliant blue and zingy yellow, make it appealing.

Granite composite, a mixture of crushed granite and resin fillers, is the most expensive—and most durable—of the composites, offering high resistance to chips, stains, scratches, and burns. It's available in a number of colors and in several neutrals.

stylish stone composites make a splash

OPPOSITE These integral sinks and counter are formed from concrete. A curved partition separates the bowls. The convenient sliding rinse board is made of stainless steel.

LEFT A white-porcelain self-rimming sink looks very much at home in a traditional kitchen.

BELOW This exposed-apron sink is mounted below the counter.

RIGHT In this example, a stainless-steel sink is undermounted in a granite countertop, an installation that's popular in both traditional and contemporary kitchen settings.

installation styles

Self-rimming (drop-in) sinks are the least costly and most common. Available in any material, they are set into the counter with the edges overlapping. The downside—crumbs, water splashes, other debris, and germs can collect along the seam of the rim.

Undermounted sinks attach below the countertop. With no visible edges, they make a smooth transition between sink and counter. To avoid warping or buckling, choose a water-resistant counter material.

Integral sinks, made of the same material as the counter, look seamless and sleek and provide no crevices where food can lodge. They can be fabricated of any moldable material, such as stainless steel, solid surfacing, composites, and concrete.

Exposed-apron sinks are undermounted but reveal the sink's front panel. They can be made from most types of sink materials.

LEFT As an alternative to a double-bowl sink, this application features two separate units, one standard size for washing and rinsing and one small size for preparing vegetables.

BELOW LEFT A roomy single-bowl sink, such as this stainless-steel model, is usually sufficient to service a small kitchen.

RIGHT An idea borrowed from restaurant kitchens, trough sinks can accommodate several cooks or cooks' helpers at the same time. This one is lined with stainless steel.

single bowl? double? what shape works for you?

BELOW RIGHT Some double-bowl sinks pair a large basin with a medium-size one, a useful configuration for some busy kitchens.

OPPOSITE FAR RIGHT In a unique installation, three separate sinks are arranged to suit the needs of the cook—a small vegetable basin is flanked by two medium-size single bowls.

bright idea

group sink

A versatile trough sink is perfect for entertaining guests in the kitchen. It can be filled with ice and used to serve chilled foods and beverages.

ABOVE A butler's pantry is a good spot for a bar sink.

RIGHT AND ABOVE RIGHT A sleek undermount sink is the centerpiece of this beverage center, which includes a wine cooler, coffeemakers, a mini-dishwasher, and storage for cups and glasses.

OPPOSITE TOP In this kitchen, the prep sink is near the action but out of the primary cook's way. For design unity, faucets for both sinks match.

OPPOSITE CENTER AND BOTTOM Bar sinks are so small that you can afford to splurge a little with a fancy faucet set or a gleaming, but delicate, hammered-copper finish.

prep and **b**ar **s**inks

In addition to the primary sink, which is the heart of the cleanup zone, prep and bar sinks are becoming standard equipment.

You'll welcome a prep sink if your kitchen is large, if two cooks often work together in it, or if you entertain frequently. Especially useful when two cooks are working simultaneously or when a dinner guest is pressed into service to scrub some vegetables or make a salad, prep sinks are placed away from the work zone. Typically drop-in or under-mount models, they are small, ranging in size from 9-in. rounds to 18-in. squares, although some are smaller. Because such a diminutive sink doesn't represent a major investment or get hard use, you can splurge a little bit on sexy materials that wouldn't hold up well in the primary work area—gleaming copper or brass, or a hand-painted ceramic or glass bowl, for example.

The popularity of bar sinks is a direct result of the kitchen's current status as a living center. With one cook busy at the main sink and a helper or two using the prep sink, a third sink where hot or cold drinks can be served is often a necessity.

standard sizes

SINK DIMENSIONS (in inches)

Sink Type	Width	Front to Rear	Basin Depth
Single-bowl	25	21–22	8–9
Double-bowl	33, 36	21–22	8–9
Side-disposal	33	21–22	8–9, 7
Triple-bowl	43	21–22	8, 6, 10
Corner	17–18 (each way)	21–11	8–9
Bar	15–25	15	5½–6

LEFT This unusual single-bowl sink sits on top of the counter.

ABOVE RIGHT The winner and still champion in popularity—the single-bowl sink that's deep enough to handle large items that don't fit in the dishwasher.

OPPOSITE TOP RIGHT A small prep sink is a big help in a busy kitchen.

BOTTOM RIGHT With a faucet at either end and work space on both sides, this trough sink is a serious cook's dream.

how to choose a kitchen sink

It's tempting to put looks first, but give some thought to your day-to-day practical needs, too. If you have a dishwasher, a large single-bowl sink may be sufficient; add a prep sink if yours is a two-cook household—but only if you have space for it. No dishwasher? You'll need a double-bowl design with equal-size basins. Other double-bowl options include one large and one medium or one small bowl. A triple-bowl sink with two deep basins for washing and rinsing and a small basin is a good choice for a kitchen with no dishwasher and no space for a separate prep sink. If you entertain, a bar sink is a bonus. Match the sink with the decor, too. Stainless steel, for example, looks good in a contemporary room, but it's also at home in any style kitchen, as are solid-surface and composite-stone designs. Porcelain sinks, in white or a pretty color, and copper sinks blend beautifully with traditional or country decors. Concrete or soapstone designs have a handsome quality. Depending on the other elements in the kitchen, they can look rustic or refined.

LEFT A contemporary-style single-lever faucet is paired with a hot water on-demand dispenser.

BELOW This pull-out spray faucet and soap dispenser boast a bronze finish.

OPPOSITE TOP For a traditional kitchen, this satin-brass faucet has a period look.

OPPOSITE BOTTOM Clean-lined, wall-mounted stainless-steel faucets harmonize with this stainless-steel sink.

Like kitchen sinks, today's faucets have a lot of panache. But, for the moment, overlook their luxurious finishes and interesting shapes, and focus on their construction. Faucets have to work hard, and you might as well buy one that will stand up well to daily wear and tear. Before you fall in love with a particular design, find out about its inner construction. The best-quality faucets are made of solid brass or a brass-base material, which are corrosion resistant. Valve construction is important as well. Ball valves ensure good quality in single-lever models, while ceramic-disk valves make single- and dual-lever faucets reliable and long lasting. Avoid faucets that use washers and plastic parts. Although these products are cheaper initially, they will cost you in repairs, and eventual replacement. Investigate finishes, too, and choose the ones that have a warranty, typically 10 years.

faucets

Faucets with pull-out spray heads are so popular today that they constitute a bona-fide kitchen trend. Other favorite built-in features may include spouts that swivel 180 degrees, antiscald mechanisms, and water filtration systems. More options, such as side-mounted sprayers, soap dispensers, and instant hot-water dispensers, are installed separately. Don't select these accessories willy-nilly. First, ask yourself if this is a feature you will really use; then make sure it matches the style and finish of your faucets and the number of holes predrilled in your sink deck. Often overlooked is the strainer and drain assembly, which you will probably have to buy separately.

installation styles

▮ **Center-set** fittings require only one drilled hole. They combine a spout and two handles set in a single base about 4 in. apart center to center. They are the least expensive installation type.

▮ **Widespread** fittings require three holes and appear to consist of three separate pieces. More costly than center-sets, these sets place hot and cold handles 8 to 12 in. apart center to center, with the spout in between.

▮ **Single-hole** fittings condense the spout and one handle for both hot and cold water into one unit.

▮ **Deck-mounted** faucets are installed on the rim of the sink or into the counter around it.

▮ **Wall-mounted** faucets are installed into the wall directly above the basin, or in the case of pot-fillers, above the cooktop. (See page 168.)

OPPOSITE TOP A center-set faucet with a swivel spout can service a two-bowl sink easily. The matching instant-water dispenser is a helpful accessory.

OPPOSITE BOTTOM LEFT This compact single-lever model is designed for a small prep sink.

OPPOSITE BOTTOM RIGHT To blend with the look of this exposed-apron sink, the homeowners chose a vintage-style, wall-mounted faucet.

RIGHT This widespread faucet set has separate hot- and cold-water valves and a coordinated side-mounted sprayer.

BELOW A deck-mounted, bridge-style fitting in gleaming polished chrome is a reproduction of a Victorian-era model.

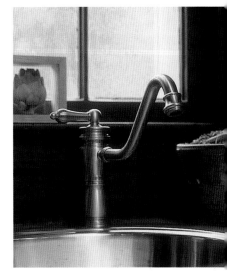

ABOVE Sculpturesque and sleek, this single-lever faucet in matte stainless steel comes equipped with a pull-out spray head.

ABOVE RIGHT A design resembling a water pump has an antique French flavor that would nicely suit an Old World or traditional kitchen setting.

RIGHT Another sleek stainless-steel model offers a built-in water filter and a separate spray attachment.

ABOVE A swan-neck spout is both graceful and practical—it allows plenty of clearance for tall pots.

RIGHT An old-fashioned chrome faucet set suits this restored vintage sink.

shop smart for shapes and styles

Today's handsome kitchen faucets are artful, resembling little kitchen sculptures. Some are dramatically contemporary, others charmingly vintage, and yet many belong to no specific design category. To maintain design unity, choose a faucet that coordinates with the overall look of your kitchen. Some will blend with elements from any style, but an ultrasleek model will look wrong amidst the coziness of a country kitchen, and vice versa. Here are other things to consider before you buy:

▌**Handle Style.** Two-handle fittings are widely available, but single handles are more effective for controlling water temperature and pressure. Lever-style or wrist-blade handles are the easiest to operate because you don't have to grip them.

▌**Spout Style.** Many designs have a standard spout that's a bit higher than the faucet base. But most people seem to prefer high-arc spouts, available in traditional or contemporary styles, because they allow clearance for large pots and platters. Some types swivel to reach both bowls in a two-basin sink.

▌**Budget.** You can buy a faucet for under a hundred dollars, but for high quality and more options you'll need to spend at least two or three times that much. Prices rise to about $1,000 for special finishes and features.

▌**Compatibility.** Buy your sink and faucets at the same time and from the same source to make sure they are compatible. Never assume faucets will fit the sink you have chosen unless your salesperson or designer has verified it.

pot fillers and sprayers

Pot fillers, borrowed from restaurant kitchens, have been a favorite feature of really serious cooks for some time, but now almost everybody wants one. These handy fittings are mounted on the wall above the range or cooktop, and they allow cooks to fill large pots with water at the site rather than lugging them, heavy and spilling over, from sink to burner. They are typically single-lever models that supply only cold water. Most of them are double-jointed, which means that they extend to reach all burners, then fold back flat against the wall when not in use. The best models have a handle at the spout as well as at the wall so that the user doesn't have to lean over hot burners to open or close the valve.

Sprays, handy for rinsing dishes, produce, and the sink basin, come in two types. **Side sprays** are sold separately and mounted next to the faucet. **Built-in, pull-out,** or **pull-down faucets** have a retractable hose and offer a high-volume spray. Hoses made of stainless steel offer the smoothest operation.

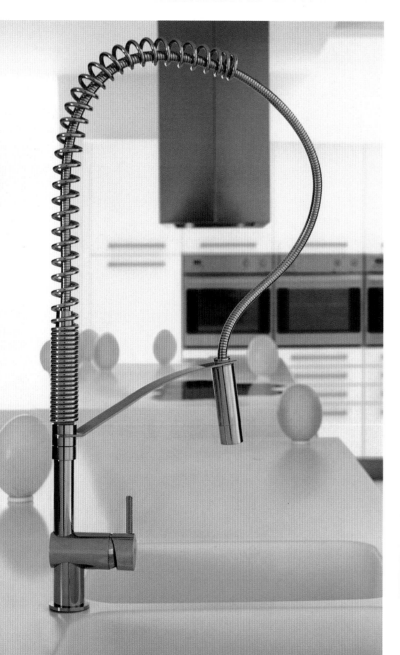

OPPOSITE FAR LEFT With the hose clipped to the base, this fitting functions as a faucet; unclipped, it becomes a sprayer that can reach beyond the sink to fill vessels on the adjacent countertop.

OPPOSITE TOP Pot fillers are a favorite feature of serious cooks. This model has a stationary spout and a crosshandle valve.

LEFT This satin-brass fitting pivots to fill pots, then folds back neatly against the wall.

ABOVE A handsome single-lever model combines a chrome body with a white-enameled pull-out spray head.

RIGHT An articulated arm on this pot filler swivels to accommodate pots on more than one burner.

ABOVE Polished copper has a glamorous gleam.

ABOVE TOP RIGHT This faucet and its accessories are finished in subtle satin nickel.

ABOVE RIGHT An antique copper finish on this gooseneck design supplies a soft patina.

RIGHT A rubbed-bronze finish is a good match for this natural stone countertop.

popular **f**inishes

There was a time when kitchen faucets were almost exclusively made of chrome. That serviceable material is still a good choice in terms of durability, tarnish resistance, and economy. But many other finishes have arrived on the scene in recent years. If you are willing to part with a little more money—and spend a little more time on maintenance—you can add a great deal of design splash to your kitchen sink.

The hot finish these days is **stainless steel,** partly because it is a good match for ever-popular pro-style appliances. It is also extremely durable and looks good with any style of faucet, contemporary or traditional. Exuding a decidedly warm, old-fashioned look, **oil-rubbed bronze, matte-finished brass,** and **antique copper** are also increasing in popularity and are considered a good complement to an Old World decor. They also pair well with stone and concrete elements. **Brass** is a perennial favorite. **Baked-on epoxy** finishes, available in a wide variety of bright colors and neutrals, can add a note of cheer to casual country-style kitchens; a black epoxy finish, on the other hand, goes with everything and coordinates well with stainless-steel and black appliances.

Satin or brushed finishes are preferred nowadays for practical and aesthetic reasons—they don't show the fingerprints and water spots that mar high-gloss faucets.

ABOVE Polished chrome has been a popular faucet finish since the turn of the century. It's suitable for vintage fittings or for the contemporary style shown here.

LEFT A black enamel finish gives this faucet a bold look and contrasts beautifully with the polished chrome water dispenser.

Thankyou Jean
For the Kitchen
That will forever
Feed My Soul

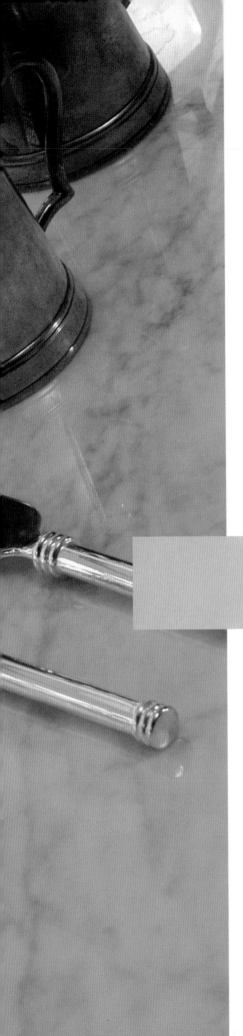

Both a design element and a work surface, the countertop is an important kitchen feature. Making a choice can be difficult—all of the options are appealing, durable, and cleanable, although some are less troublesome than others. If you're a serious cook, you may want a tough surface that doesn't need a lot of care. If your countertops will be a major design feature, look for a material that commands attention. When you're ready to shop, remember to take cabinets and flooring samples with you.

Countertops

I stone I solid surfacing I
I tile I plastic laminate I concrete I
I wood and metal I

Although they must be periodically sealed for protection, countertops made of marble offer a distinctive look in formal, traditional-style kitchens.

I f you're considering a stone countertop, you already know that granite is king. Beautiful and luminous, it makes a strong design statement and looks great in traditional or contemporary kitchens. Although granite is the hardest, most durable, and least scratch-able of the stones, it is porous and stains easily. To maintain its luminosity, you must seal it right after installation and reseal it often. Granite is expensive, and it's heavy, requiring more support than standard cabinet framing provides.

stone

Marble, another beautiful stone, is seldom used on serious work counters because oils, tomatoes, and other acidic substances readily stain its porous surface. Instead, use it in a baking area, where its cool surface is ideal, or in another part of your kitchen that doesn't see much action. Frequent sealing helps prevent stains, but most people aren't willing to do that much maintenance. Like marble, limestone is soft and susceptible to staining, but homeowners are choosing it anyway. Seduced by its creamy-beige tones and weathered-looking surface, some people like the character that comes with imperfection.

Slate is less porous, durable, and requires no sealing. It's available in black, gray, and shades of green and red. Like all stone, it looks luxurious but can scratch and chip easily. Soapstone is enjoying a resurgence. It stands up to heavy use and ages to a charcoal gray.

BELOW LEFT Granite is available in dozens of colors, and it may be more resistant to bacteria than most other materials.

BELOW RIGHT Polished granite resists scratches and stains, making it a favorite of serious cooks.

RIGHT Distinctive veining and coloring gives this marble countertop a unique appearance.

OPPOSITE BOTTOM LEFT Although less durable than granite, the matte-like finish of slate is a handsome alternative to polished stone.

OPPOSITE BOTTOM RIGHT Because dough will not stick to it, consider using a marble countertop or marble inset in a bake center.

ABOVE As with solid surfacing and natural stone, quartz composite countertops work well with undermounted sinks.

RIGHT This blue composite countertop brightens up a white kitchen while providing another work surface.

OPPOSITE ABOVE A closer look at the blue composite reveals color speckles that add the depth and texture of lapis to a countertop.

OPPOSITE BOTTOM Add pizzazz with a zesty red composite countertop.

engineered (composite) stone

Produced by binding stone chips—predominantly quartz—to powders and resins, engineered stone (also called *composite material*) is an extremely hard and durable material that is becoming a popular choice for kitchen counters. Because it offers a textured and speckled or variegated look, it somewhat resembles natural stone, but its patterns are more uniform and consistent and the spectrum of colors is larger. Several companies are manufacturing engineered stone, and

their color palettes generally include earth tones—ranging from light to dark, rich shades—and colors, including a couple of deep reds and bright blues and yellows definitely not found in nature. Engineered stone cleans easily and is heat, scratch, and stain resistant. It doesn't need to be sealed, polished, or otherwise specially treated. It's almost as expensive as stone but may be worth the money if you're after low maintenance and a more uniform look than natural stone can offer.

bright idea

thumbs up

Solid-surfacing pullout shelves with dividers are perfect for a gardening area.

solid-

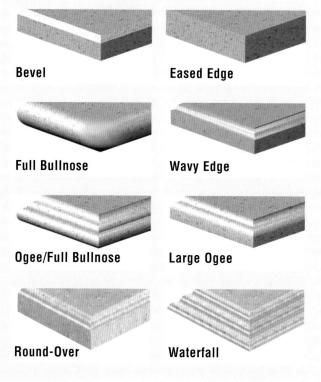

edge treatments

Select an edge treatment for your countertop that matches the kitchen's architectural style.

Bevel

Eased Edge

Full Bullnose

Wavy Edge

Ogee/Full Bullnose

Large Ogee

Round-Over

Waterfall

surface material

Somewhat less expensive than natural stone or the composite materials, solid surfacing is a man-made, nonporous product. Made of filled acrylic and polyester polymers, the material can be used to form a countertop with an integral sink for an elegant seamless appearance. It can also be carved and finished with interesting architectural edges. (See "Edge Treatments," above.) For an especially distinguished look, solid-surfacing countertop edges can be inlaid with wood, metal, or a contrasting color strip. Another attractive feature of the material is the wide variety of colors and patterns that are available. The stone look-alikes are the best known, but solid surfacing also comes in white, a variety of off-whites, pastel and primary colors, and earth tones. As a countertop, it performs well, resisting stains, moisture, and standing up well to general kitchen wear and tear. It's easy to clean, too; abrasive cleansers can be safely used. Solid-surfacing countertops are not impervious to burns or scratches, but because the color goes all the way through the material, these marks can be buffed or sanded out successfully. It is best to trust this process to a professional fabricator. The cost of a solid-surface countertop can be comparable to some stones, although certain colors are more affordable.

OPPOSITE TOP A creamy white countertop coordinates well with these light wood cabinets.

OPPOSITE BOTTOM LEFT A vibrant green was selected for the countertop and pullouts in a potting bench.

LEFT The nature of solid surfacing makes a variety of decorative edge treatments possible.

ABOVE LEFT Solid surfacing can imitate the look of natural stone.

Like stone, ceramic tile is an age-old, durable material. It is available in a huge variety of price ranges, colors, patterns, sizes, and shapes—from tiny hexagonal mosaics to large 12- or 18-inch squares. With this variety, there is no end to the one-of-a-kind designs that you can create with tile. Trim pieces, relief designs, and decorative inserts are also available to heighten the interesting effects and mimic architectural detailing. Because there are so many colors and patterns and so many ways to combine them, a tile countertop can be designed to suit any kitchen style, whether it be sleek and streamlined, sophisticated and dignified, or casual and colorful. Glazed tiles **tile** shrug off burns, scratches, and stains. However, they can crack if you drop something on them—and whatever you drop will almost certainly break, too. Unglazed tiles offer a rustic look that some people like, but they are porous, which means that they need frequent sealing to keep stains and germs at bay.

Ceramic tile is easy to keep clean, but the grout between the tiles can be a problem. You can clean the grout lines periodically with a mild bleach solution or use a dark-colored grout in a shade that matches or contrasts with the tile. Always seal grout to prevent bacteria and other germs from seeping into the material. Some grouts come conveniently premixed with a sealer.

OPPOSITE TOP AND RIGHT Copper accent tiles add warmth and charm to a neutral ceramic tile countertop.

OPPOSITE BOTTOM LEFT AND RIGHT A carved-wood edge treatment beautifully accents these luminous glass tiles.

ABOVE Black and white tiles create an eye-catching backsplash.

LEFT White tiles create a smooth visual transition between the countertop and backsplash.

LEFT Ceramic tiles provide an easy-clean area around a cooktop.

RIGHT A mural made of tiny mosaic tiles adds interest to a neutral-color backsplash above the cooktop.

LEFT CENTER A festive, multi-color tile backsplash shows the versatility of ceramic tiles. Note the raised-tile band between the areas of color.

BELOW LEFT AND RIGHT Tiles add distinction to any kitchen. Here are two examples that show the full-range of what is possible. To the right, a hand-painted trompe l'oeil design adds whimsy to the wall behind a counter. To the left, a mosaic-tile mural is the focal point of this kitchen.

backsplashes

Backsplashes have come a long way, from insignificant little shields that protected the walls behind the sink and cooktop to significant design elements. And because the space they occupy is proportionately small, you can afford to splurge a little, selecting a luxurious material that might be too pricey or too delicate in larger doses. If you're after a unified look, you can continue the countertop material right up the backsplash. Looking for a little more excitement? Try tile laid out in an interesting pattern. In some kitchens, the cooktop backsplash is devoted to an elaborate tile mural. Want more razzle-dazzle? Choose shiny copper, retro-style quilted stainless steel, shimmering glass tiles, sections of mirror, or a mix of materials. In a family-oriented kitchen, cork backsplashes furnish a place to tack family photos, mementos, messages, and the like. The sky's the limit, but stick with an easy-to-clean material behind the sink and cooktop—spatters and splashes are inevitable.

ABOVE An abstract of relief tiles above the sink stands out as a work of art on a neutral backsplash.

BELOW Even when confined to the 18 to 24 in. of a common backsplash area, you can create a variety of custom designs with versatile tile.

LEFT You can order a plastic laminate counter built to your specifications. Most fabricators offer a variety of edge treatments.

BELOW LEFT The neutral color and the low-sheen finish on this plastic laminate countertop resembles a soft brushed stone.

BELOW A standard plastic laminate countertop has seams that are visible along the edges.

LEFT Use a cutting board to keep from scratching the finish on this countertop.

BELOW Advanced engineering makes it possible to realistically mimic the look of natural stone in plastic laminate.

plastic laminate

Unless you choose a fancy edge treatment—a contrasting color, a bevel, or a wood or metal inlay—plastic laminate is your best bet for kitchen-counter economy. Other positive aspects of this versatile material include quick and straightforward installation, easy cleanup, and an infinite variety of colors, textures, and patterns, including stone, wood, and metal look-alikes. A new plastic laminate pattern designed to mimic ceramic tile comes complete with indentations that resemble grout lines. But you'll have to be careful not to stain, scorch, chip, or scratch this material. These blemishes cannot be satisfactorily repaired. And you'll need to be vigilant about water, too—don't let it collect, especially near seams where it can warp or cause the material to lift off its substrate. However, plastic laminate comes in different grades and is usually affordable to replace. A post-formed countertop, which comes with an integral backsplash and a rounded edge, is even more economical. The color selection for these ready-made counters is limited and the plastic laminate is thinner so it's more susceptible to damage. But you will get a few good years out of it—and the price is right. Keep in mind that spots and smudges stand out sharply on a glossy-finish plastic laminate; matte or textured finishes are better for camouflaging wear and tear.

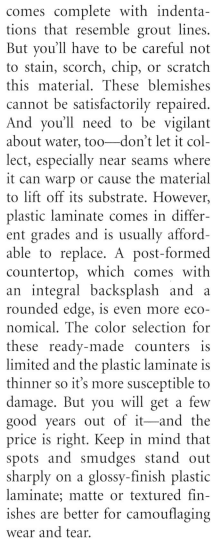

concrete

Once considered daring and avant-garde, concrete counters are moving into the mainstream. And it's no wonder—concrete is an intriguing and versatile material that can be formed into any number of interesting shapes. It's a natural choice for an integral counter-and-sink installation. Just right for ultra-contemporary, minimalist kitchens, concrete also provides a mellow weathered look that works well with country or European-farmhouse styles.

Concrete is often used in its natural state, a gray hue that mellows over time, but if that look reminds you too much of a sidewalk or a garage floor, try a tint. Any number of colors are available—earthy tones such as ivory, clay, or beige; pastels; or vivid and deeply saturated shades. Finishes vary from highly textured to rough or rustic; glossy and polished to subdued and low sheen. This unusual material takes on an even more individualistic appearance inlaid with small stones, bits of shiny metal, or colored glass.

Concrete counters are resistant to heat and scratching, but because they are porous they can stain readily and require periodic sealing. All of this versatility and uniqueness comes with a high price tag. Concrete itself is not expensive, but fabrication is difficult and time consuming and requires an expert. If poorly or hastily prepared, your concrete counter will surely crack. It's a good idea to get references from the installer and check out previous installations that have been in place for some time.

ABOVE Concrete may be the most versatile of all countertop surface materials because it can be molded into any shape you desire.

RIGHT Concrete countertops are either precast before a job, or they are created on site.

ABOVE The versatility of concrete is evident in this polished counter, matching sink, and integral backsplash.

BELOW LEFT As you probably guessed, concrete is durable. It is the strongest of the natural surfaces.

BELOW RIGHT As with other countertop options, concrete is available in a variety of colors.

ABOVE LEFT The rich chocolate-colored stain on the wood countertops in this kitchen camouflages spills and splatters.

ABOVE RIGHT Most people select stainless steel for its sleek modern looks, but it pairs beautifully with white marble in this Victorian kitchen.

LEFT Solid maple on this island counter coordinates with the kitchen cabinetry.

wood and metal

Despite its vulnerability to moisture, scratches, and stains, wood, especially butcher block, remains popular. Its warm look is particularly suitable for country or traditional kitchens. Hardwood counters are easy to work on and relatively easy to maintain. Pools of water will do damage, however, if not wiped up right away. Your wood counter will eventually show stains and scratches. Some cooks like this well-used look, but if you don't agree you can periodically sand out imperfections and reseal the wood with nontoxic mineral oil.

Recent studies have shown that wood is a sanitary material with inherent properties that protect it from built-up bacteria. Metal is also sanitary, and the only countertop material that can be safely cleaned with bleach. A great addition to a trendy pro-style kitchen or a minimalist design, metal counters—usually stainless steel—are popular options. Stainless steel is impervious to heat, water, and stains. It can be formed into an integral sink and countertop configuration and is extremely durable (the lower the gauge, the thicker the material). On the down side, it's expensive and noisy to work on unless it's cushioned with extra plywood. A satin or brushed finish can disguise some of the scratches that come with time and use.

LEFT Sealed with a food-safe varnish for easy maintenance, this butcher block is a perfect surface for chopping produce or slicing bread or cheese.

BELOW Stainless steel on the counters and backsplash complements the pro-style range and the contemporary look of this kitchen.

W hether you're remodeling an old kitchen or building a new one, abundant light should be high on the list of the features you will incorporate. Without it, a kitchen isn't pleasant, efficient, or safe. In fact, lack of light is one of the reasons homeowners decide to remodel. So why do many people often fail to plan for it? Tackle the question now, while you are still in the planning stages. As you will see, there are many ways to introduce natural and artificial light to make your kitchen inviting and functional.

Light Your Kitchen

I natural light I
I artificial light I

During the day, several types of windows usher sunshine into this kitchen. After dark, a combination of several types of fixtures keep the brightness going.

A single window over the sink and a pane of glass in the top half of the back door—sound familiar? Until recently, that scenario represented the extent of natural lighting in many kitchens. Fortunately, that picture has changed. Nowadays, architects, interior designers, and remodeling contractors are well versed in window technology and can help you bring abundant natural light into your new kitchen and establish a connection

natural light

with the outdoors, too. If you're starting from scratch, plan the windows early in the process, when you are laying out the food-preparation and eating zones. If you're remodeling, look for ways to enlarge existing windows or seek out likely places to install new ones. Replacing dated windows with larger, more interesting units can introduce more light and at the same time make the kitchen more appealing. You might also consider adding windows or glass doors that overlook the garden, or installing a greenhouse window above the

sink to supply sunshine and a spot to grow herbs year-round.

Before you commit to any new windows, ask yourself two questions. One, what kind of view will they provide? If you won't be looking at something pleasant, try a different location or consider a skylight, which maximizes sunlight but circumvents ugly views. Two, will your new windows harmonize with the architecture of the house?

ABOVE A clever way to gain light—replace a backsplash with small windows.

RIGHT Divided-lite windows in this eating area harmonize with the architecture.

FAR RIGHT Artificial and natural light strike a perfect balance.

skylights and roof windows

According to some lighting experts, skylights supply up to 30 percent more light than vertical windows; and they also make the room feel larger.

Skylights, installed along a roof slope or on a flat roof, are generally not reachable. However, venting, or operable, skylights, hinged at the top, can be opened by an electric wall switch, motorized or manual hand-crank, or remote control device to provide fresh air and ventilation and to let hot summer air escape. Fixed skylights do not open.

Roof windows (the term is sometimes used interchangeably with operable skylight) are generally set lower in the roofline than skylights and are reachable. Sashes are designed to pivot so that the outside glass can be cleaned from inside the house.

To save money on energy bills, choose skylights and roof windows with insulated thermal glass, which will minimize heat loss in winter and cut down on heat gain in summer. Another way to combat heat gain is to shade skylights during the hottest part of the day. Skylight manufacturers offer blinds and shades as accessories. Using skylights with tinted glass is another way to reduce heat gain.

OPPOSITE BELOW The slope of a cathedral ceiling is an ideal location for a row of room-brightening sky-lights or roof windows.

LEFT A charming little window is sufficient to illuminate this bar area.

ABOVE Pouring in through divided-lite windows, sunshine brightens a dining area, then spills over into the nearby food-prep zone.

RIGHT Skylights work in conjunction with a vertical window to bathe this work area in daylight.

To create a welcoming—and safe—environment in your kitchen you will need artificial lighting in three categories. General, or ambient, lighting creates a comfortable level of brightness without being obvious about it—like a woman whose makeup is applied skillfully: she looks good but you can't pinpoint exactly why. Task lighting, crucial for efficiency and safety, should be installed everywhere there is close work done in the kitchen. Many people overlook accent lighting, but it, too, is important. By focusing attention on particular elements, say a shelf of pretty collectibles, you'll enhance the appeal of your kitchen. The bulbs you choose are also important. Incandescent bulbs emit a warm light. They don't cost much initially but eat up energy and generate heat. A more energy-efficient choice, warm-white fluorescent bulbs cast a shadowless, diffuse light, render colors and textures accurately, and are effective for general or task lighting. Halogen bulbs produce a whiter, brighter light. They are costly, however, and even the low-voltage type burn hotly and emit UV rays. New krypton and xenon bulbs are cooler, brighter, and most efficient.

artificial light

fixture types

Suspended globes, chandeliers, and pendants can light up an entire a room or a particular task area. Hang them 12–20 in. below an 8-ft. ceiling or 30–36 in. above the tops of tables and counters.

Surface-mount fixtures attach directly to the ceiling or wall (sconces). Most distribute very even, shadowless general lighting. To minimize glare, surface-mount fixtures should be shielded. Fixtures with sockets for several smaller bulbs distribute more even lighting than those with just one or two large bulbs.

Recessed fixtures are mounted inside the ceiling or soffit. They include fixed and aimable incandescent downlights, shielded fluorescent tubes, and totally luminous ceilings. Recessed fixtures require up to twice as much wattage as surface-mount and suspended types.

Track lights, including bendable cable systems, can be used for general, task, or accent lighting—or any combination of the three. You can select from a broad array of modular fixtures, clip them anywhere along a track, and revise your lighting scheme any time you like. Locate tracks 12–24 in. out from the edges of wall cabinets to minimize shadows on countertops.

Undercabinet compact fluorescent strips or incandescent fixtures mounted to the undersides of wall cabinets can bathe counters with sufficient task lighting. It's important to illuminate at least two-thirds of the counter's length.

Cove lights reflect upward to the ceiling, creating smooth and even general lighting or dramatic architectural effects. Consider locating custom cove lights on top of wall cabinets in the space normally occupied by soffits.

ABOVE LEFT AND LEFT In this suburban kitchen, a skillful lighting plan creates warmth and efficiency. A handsome suspended fixture and recessed downlights provide overall illumination, while undercabinet task lights brighten the cooktop and work counters.

general lighting

General, or ambient, lighting fills your entire kitchen, creating a warm and welcoming backdrop, both day and night. No matter how much natural light pours in, you will have to supplement it electrically on cloudy days; a well-balanced lighting scheme will duplicate the sunny glow of daylight. Sources for ambient light include ceiling fixtures, cabinet uplights, recessed downlights, wall sconces, even table lamps. Whatever your light sources, equip them with dimming features so that you can adjust brightness levels. You'll want bright light for working and seeing into cabinets and drawers, and softer, cozier illumination for dining. In today's open-plan homes, dimmers are also handy for coordinating kitchen lighting with adjacent rooms such as dining or living spaces or family rooms. Some lighting specialists even recommend that every light in the kitchen have its own circuit, which allows you to create the ambiance you want by adjusting lights individually. Space your fixtures so that they supply an even spread of light. If illumination breaks into a discernable pattern, you'll know that the light sources are placed too far apart.

Your color scheme will affect your lighting choices, as will the size and shape of the room. Light-colored or high-gloss cabinets, counters, and other surfaces reflect light, requiring less illumination than a room with dark or matte-finished surfaces. With high ceilings you'll need bright lights to dispel shadows. With lower ceilings, it's best to reduce brightness because light bounces off low ceilings and walls. The number of windows and the way they are oriented will also affect your lighting requirements.

Keep style in mind when you shop for fixtures. Recessed downlights, which are unobtrusive, will fit with any design scheme, but suspended fixtures, sconces, and track lights should match the look of your room. You'll have a wealth of designs from which to choose. Finishes for fixtures run the gamut, from enameled colors to shiny, matte, and antiqued metal patinas.

LEFT For general illumination, this kitchen relies on some daylight, recessed ceiling fixtures, and a pendant light over the work island.

BELOW AND ALL VIEWS OPPOSITE Several types of fixtures supplement natural light and enliven the design of this kitchen. A chandelier hangs over the dining table; sconces call attention to the architecture of the window; and period-style pendants brighten the work counter. A surprise touch—the pretty table lamp shining on the sink.

RIGHT Strips of low-voltage task lights illuminate work counters in the corner of this kitchen.

BELOW Sconces fitted with compact fluorescent tubes brighten cooking and cleanup zones. Energy-efficient fluorescent lights are bright but not hot the way some incandescent lights are. They make economic sense in a room where lights stay on for long periods.

BELOW RIGHT Low-voltage xenon lights shine brightly on a work counter.

OPPOSITE ABOVE Some ventilation systems come with built-in compact lights.

lighting **w**ork **a**reas

Any work you do in the kitchen—slicing, sautéing, rinsing, washing, even reading recipes or the newspaper—requires at least 100 watts of incandescent (or 60 watts of fluorescent) light. For countertop work areas, undercabinet lighting is the most effective. This type of light, whether fluorescent strips, miniature track lights, or a low-voltage linear system, should be installed close to the front edge of the wall cabinet so that it will bathe your counters in the kind of bright light you need for close work. The cooking and cleanup zones will also need effective task lighting. Undercabinet strips or recessed downlights are often used to illuminate the sink, and some range hoods come with built-in lighting for the cooktop. Track lighting. recessed fixtures, or pendants are popular choices to brighten work islands. If you will be using recessed ceiling fixtures or spots to light a work counter, place them two feet away from the wall—otherwise you'll be standing in your own shadow while you work.

Does your kitchen include an eating area? If so, dim the undercabinet lighting, or turn it off completely, when it's time to eat so that it doesn't shine right into people's eyes. Another tip—install a separate switch for each task light so that you can turn them off whenever you like.

pendants and **c**handeliers

In the kitchen, pendants and chandeliers can supply all three types of lighting—overall, task, and accent—but they're most often used for ambient light over the dining table, a booth, an island, or any place family and friends gather to have their meals. If your kitchen ceiling is a conventional 8 ft. high, lighting specialists suggest that your suspended fixture be installed so that the bottom hangs from 27–36 in. above a dining table. Raise the height 3 in. for every additional foot of ceiling height. One or more decorative pendants over a booth will provide bright task light; dimmed for dining, they'll emit a more intimate glow. If you choose a pendant that is open at the bottom, such as a Tiffany-style fixture, make sure the top of the fixture allows some light to escape upward, as well. To eliminate glare underneath, use a diffusing bowl or disk, or a semi-opaque bulb. Also, never use a fixture with an exposed bulb. Be aware that a hanging fixture may also create a harsh glare over a glass table.

Suspended over work islands, chandeliers and pendants are stylish sources of task light for food-preparation chores. Turned up high, these same fixtures may provide sufficient overall illumination for a small kitchen; dimmed they make a decorative kitchen focal point.

LEFT Period-style pendants suit this traditional kitchen.

BELOW LEFT A sleek pendant fixture brightens a corner.

ABOVE Unusual tear-drop pendants supply light and style.

ABOVE RIGHT In a French-inspired design, this chandelier is an enlightened addition.

RIGHT A pendant supplies task light over a work area.

bright idea

nifty fixture

Pendant fixtures with retractable cords can stay above it all for overall lighting or move close for cozy dining.

ABOVE Candle sconces on either side of the windows draw attention to handsome architectural details.

LEFT The chandelier over this dining table is fitted with candles, which provide the most flattering illumination of all.

OPPOSITE TOP LEFT Tiny interior lights showcase collectibles in display cabinets located in the soffit.

OPPOSITE BOTTOM LEFT Small spotlights on a shapely track can be focused on wall art or work surfaces.

OPPOSITE TOP RIGHT An adjustable cable system takes care of both ambient and task lighting.

track and accent lights

Track lighting is especially helpful in the kitchen. The "track," a surface-mounted channel that holds the lights and brings power to them, can be installed overhead to encompass the general area you want to illuminate. Individual lights can then be attached to the track to shine specifically where you want them and can easily be moved should you revise your lighting plan. Although track lighting was originally introduced into modern kitchens, individual fixtures come in a wide variety of sizes from miniature to major, and in styles from contemporary to traditional. In a modern kitchen, the track system often serves as a design feature, but in more traditional rooms, attention is directed not to the track itself but to what it's lighting. In a modest-sized kitchen, tracks can provide both ambient and task illumination, but because they are basically directional, in larger rooms they perform best as task or accent lighting. It's tricky to get track lighting just right. Ask your architect, interior designer, or a lighting specialist for help with the design.

Use accent lighting to call attention to an interesting element or focal point in your kitchen, such as a good-looking range hood, a tile mural above the cooktop, or an exposed brick wall. Sconces, directional track lights, or strip lights can all be employed to accent a decorative feature, and a table lamp might even be used to call attention to a beautiful cabinet or hutch.

Resource Guide

MANUFACTURERS

Above View
4750 South 10th St.
Milwaukee, WI 53221
414-744-7118
www.aboveview.com
Makes ornamental ceiling tiles.

Amana
403 West 4th St.
Newton, IA 50208
800-843-0304
www.amana.com
Manufactures refrigerators, dishwashers, and cooking appliances.

American Standard
P.O. Box 6820
1 Centennial Plaza
Piscataway, NJ 08855-6820
www.americanstandard-us.com
Manufactures plumbing and tile products.

Armstrong World Industries
2500 Columbia Ave.
P.O. Box 3001
Lancaster, PA 17604
717-397-0611
www.armstrong.com
Manufactures floors, cabinets, ceilings, and ceramic tiles.

Bach Faucets
19701 DaVinci
Lake Forest, CA 92610
866-863-6584
www.bachfaucet.com
Manufactures faucets.

Big Chill Refrigerators
877-842-3269
www.bigchillfridge.com
Manufactures retro-style refrigerators.

Blanco America
110 Mount Holly By-Pass
Lumberton, NJ 08048
www.blancoamerica.com
Manufactures sinks and faucets.

Bosch Home Appliances
5551 McFadden Ave.
Huntington Beach, CA 92807
714-901-6600

The following list of manufacturers and associations is meant to be a general guide to additional industry and product-related sources. It is not intended as a listing of products and manufacturers represented by the photographs in this book.

www.boschappliances.com

Manufactures major and small appliances.

Bruce Hardwood Floors, a div. of Armstrong World Industries

www.bruce.com

Manufactures hardwood flooring.

Corian, a div. of DuPont

800-426-7426

www.corian.com

Manufactures solid surfacing.

Crossville, Inc.

P.O. Box 1168

Crossville, TN 38557

931-484-2110

www.crossvilleinc.com

Manufactures porcelain, stone, and metal tile.

Delta Faucet Company

55 East 111th St.

P.O. Box 40980

Indianapolis, IN 46280

800-345-3358

www.deltafaucet.com

Manufactures faucets.

Dex Studios

404-753-0600

www.dexstudios.com

Creates custom concrete sinks and countertops.

Elkay

2222 Camden Ct.

Oak Brook, IL 60523

630-574-8484

www.elkayusa.com

Manufactures sinks, faucets, and countertops.

Fisher and Paykel

www.fisherandpaykel.com

Manufactures kitchen appliances.

Formica Corporation

10155 Reading Rd.

Cincinnati, OH 45241

513-786-3525

www.formica.com

Manufactures plastic laminate and solid surfacing.

Resource Guide

General Electric

580-634-0151

www.ge.com

Manufactures appliances and electronics.

Glidden

800-454-3336

www.glidden.com

Manufactures paint.

Hartco, a div. of Armstrong World Industries

www.hartco.com

Manufactures hardwood flooring.

Jenn-Air, a div. of the Maytag Corp.

240 Edwards St.

Cleveland, TN 37311

800-688-1100

www.jennair.com

Manufactures major cooking and small appliances.

Kohler

800-456-4537

www.kohler.com

Manufactures plumbing products.

KraftMaid Cabinetry

P.O. Box 1055

15535 South State Ave.

Middlefield, OH 44062

440-632-5333

www.kraftmaid.com

Manufactures cabinetry.

LG

1000 Sylvan Ave.

Englewood Cliffs, NJ 07632

800-243-0000

www.lge.com

Manufactures major appliances.

Maytag Corp.

800-688-9900

www.maytag.com

Manufactures major appliances.

MGS Progetti

www.mgsprogetti.com

Manufactures faucets.

Miele

www.miele.com

Manufactures major appliances.

Moen

25300 Al Moen Dr.

North Olmsted, OH 44070

800-289-6636

www.moen.com

Manufactures plumbing products.

Native Trails

800-786-0862

www.nativetrails.net

A source for handcrafted copper sinks and Talavera tiles.

Plain and Fancy Custom Cabinetry

Oak St and Route 501

Schaeffertown, PA 17088

800-447-9006

www.plainfancycabinetry.com

Makes custom cabinetry.

Price Pfister, Inc.

19701 Da Vinci

Foothill Ranch, CA 92610

800-732-8238

www.pricepfister.com

Manufactures faucets.

Robbins, a div. of Armstrong World Industries

www.robbins.com

Makes hardwood flooring.

Sherwin-Williams

www.sherwinwilliams.com

Manufactures paint.

Sonoma Cast Stone

P.O. Box 1721

Sonoma, CA 95476

888-807-4234

www.sonomastone.com

Designs and builds concrete sinks and countertops.

Resource Guide

Sub-Zero Freezer Co.

P.O. Box 44130

Madison, WI 53744

800-222-7820

www.subzero.com

Manufactures professional-style refrigeration appliances.

Thibaut Inc.

480 Frelinghuysen Ave.

Newark, NJ 07114

800-223-0704

www.thibautdesign.com

Manufactures wallpaper and fabrics.

Viking Range Corp.

111 Front St.

Greenwood, MS 38930

www.vikingrange.com

Manufactures professional-style kitchen appliances.

Wilsonart International

P.O. Box 6110

Temple, TX 76503

800-433-3222

www.wilsonart.com

Manufactures plastic laminate countertops.

**Wolf Appliance Company,
a div. of Sub-Zero Freezer Co.**

www.wolfappliance.com

Manufactures professional-style cooking appliances.

Wood-Mode Fine Custom Cabinetry

1 Second St.

Kreamer, PA 17833

877-635-7500

www.wood-mode.com

Manufactures custom cabinetry for the kitchen.

Zodiaq, a div. of DuPont

800-426-7426

www.zodiaq.com

Manufactures quartz-composite countertops and sinks.

ASSOCIATIONS

National Association of Remodeling Industry (NARI)

780 Lee St., Ste. 200

Des Plaines, IL 60016

800-611-6274

www.nari.org

A professional organization for remodelers, contractors, and design-build professionals.

National Kitchen and Bath Association (NKBA)

687 Willow Grove St.

Hackettstown, NJ 07840

800-652-2776

www.nkba.org

A national trade organization for kitchen and bath design professionals. It offers consumers product information and a referral service.

Tile Council Of America

100 Clemson Research Blvd.

Anderson, SC 29625

864-646-8453

www.tileusa.com

A trade organization dedicated to promoting the tile industry. It also provides consumer information on selecting and installing tile.

Glossary

Accent lighting: A type of light that highlights an area or object to emphasize that aspect of a room's character.

Accessible design: Design that accommodates persons with physical disabilities.

Adaptable design: Design that can be easily changed to accommodate a person with disabilities.

Ambient light: General illumination that surrounds a room. There is no visible source of the light.

Appliance garage: Countertop storage for small appliances.

Apron: The front panel of a sink that may or may not be exposed.

Awning window: A window with a single framed-glass panel. It is hinged at the top to swing out when it is open.

Backlighting: Illumination coming from a source behind or at the side of an object.

Backsplash: The finish material that covers the wall behind a countertop. The backsplash can be attached to the countertop or separate from it.

Baking center: An area near an oven(s) and a refrigerator that contains a countertop for rolling out dough and storage for baking supplies.

Base cabinet: A cabinet that rests on the floor under a countertop.

Base plan: A map of an existing room that shows detailed measurements and the location of fixtures, appliances, and other permanent elements.

Basin: A shallow sink.

Built-in: A cabinet, shelf, medicine chest, or other storage unit that is recessed into the wall.

Bump out: Living space created by cantilevering the floor and ceiling joists (or adding to a floor slab) and extending the exterior wall of a room.

Butcher block: A counter or table-top material composed of strips of hardwood, often rock maple, laminated together and sealed against moisture.

Carousel shelves: The front extension of a bathtub that runs from the rim to floor.

Casement window: A window that consists of one framed-glass panel that is hinged on the side. It swings outward from the opening at the turn of a crank.

Centerline: The dissecting line through the center of an object, such as a sink.

CFM: An abbreviation that refers to the amount of cubic feet of air that is moved per minute by an exhaust fan.

Chair rail: A decorative wall molding installed midway between the floor and ceiling. Traditionally, chair rails protected walls from damage from chair backs.

Cleanup center: The area of a kitchen where the sink, waste-disposal unit, trash compactor, dishwasher, and related accessories are grouped for easy access and efficient use.

Code: A locally or nationally enforced mandate regarding structural design, materials, plumbing, or electrical systems that states what you can or cannot do when you build or remodel. Codes are intended to protect standards of health, safety, and land use.

Combing: A painting technique that involves using a small device with teeth or grooves over a wet painted surface to create a grained effect.

Cooking center: The kitchen area where the cooktop, oven(s), and food preperation surfaces, appliances, and utensils are grouped.

Countertop: The work surface of a counter, island, or peninsula, usually 36 inches high. Common countertop materials include plastic laminate, ceramic tile, slate, and solid surfacing.

Cove lights: Lights that reflect upward, sometimes located on top of wall cabinets.

Crown molding: A decorative molding usually installed where the wall and ceiling meet.

Dimmer Switch: A switch that can vary the intensity of the light source that it controls.

Double-hung window: A window that consists of two framed-glass panels that slide open vertically, guided by a metal or wood track.

Downlighting: A lighting technique that illuminates objects or areas from above.

Duct: A tube or passage for venting indoor air to the outside.

Faux painting: Various painting techniques that mimic wood, marble, and other stone.

Fittings: The plumbing devices that transport water to the fixtures. These can include faucets, sprayers, and spouts. Also pertains to hardware and some accessories, such as soap dispensers and instant-water dispensers.

Fixed window: A window that cannot be opened. It is usually a decorative unit, such as a half-round or Palladian-style window.

Fixture: Any fixed part of the structural design, such as sinks.

Fluorescent lamp: An energy-efficient light source made of a tube with an interior phosphorus coating that glows when energized by electricity.

Framed cabinets: Cabinets with a full frame across the face of the cabinet box.

Frameless cabinets: European-style cabinets without a face frame.

Full bath: A bath that includes a toilet, lavatory, and bathing fixtures, such as a tub or shower.

Glass blocks: Decorative building blocks made of translucent glass used for nonload-bearing walls to allow passage of light.

Glazing (walls): A technique for applying a thinned, tinted wash of translucent color to a dry undercoat of paint.

Ground-fault circuit interrupter (GFCI): A safety circuit breaker that compares the amount of current entering a receptacle with the amount leaving. If there is a discrepancy of 0.005 volt, the GFCI breaks the circuit in a fraction of a second. GFCIs are required by the National Electrical Code in areas that are subject to dampness.

Grout: A binder and filler applied in the joints between ceramic tile.

Glossary

Halogen bulb: A bulb filled with halogen gas, a substance that causes the particles of tungsten to be redeposited onto the tungsten filament. This process extends the lamp's life and makes the light whiter and brighter.

Highlight: The lightest tone in a room.

Incandescent lamp: A bulb that contains a conductive filament through which current flows. The current reacts with an inert gas inside the bulb, which makes the filament glow.

Intensity: Strength of a color.

Island: A base cabinet and countertop unit that stands independent from walls so that there is access from all four sides.

Joist: Set in a parallel fashion, these framing members support the boards of a ceiling or a floor.

Kitchen fans: Fans that remove grease, moisture, smoke, and heat from the kitchen.

Lazy Susan: Axis-mounted shelves that revolve. Also called carousel shelves.

Load-bearing wall: A wall that supports a structure's vertical load. Openings in any load-bearing wall must be reinforced to carry the live and dead weight of the structure's load.

Low-voltage lights: Lights that operate on 12 to 50 volts rather than the standard 120 volts used in most homes.

Muntins: Framing members of a window that divide the panes of glass.

Nonbearing wall: An interior wall that provides no structural support for any portion of the house.

Palette: A range of colors that complement one another.

Peninsula: A countertop, with or without a base cabinet, that is connected at one end to a wall or another countertop and extends outward, providing access on three sides.

Proportion: The relationship of one object to another.

Recessed light fixtures: Light fixtures that are installed into ceilings, soffits, or cabinets and are flush with the surrounding area.

Refacing: Replacing the doors and drawers on cabinets and covering the frame with a matching material.

Roof window: A horizontal window that is installed on the roof. Roof windows are ventilating.

Scale: The size of a room or object.

Sconce: A decorative wall bracket, sometimes made of iron or glass, that shields a bulb.

Secondary work center: An area of the kitchen where extra activity is done, such as laundry or baking.

Semicustom cabinets: Cabinets that are available in specific sizes but with a wide variety of options.

Sight line: The natural line of sight the eye travels when looking into or around a room.

Skylight: A framed opening in the roof that admits sunlight into the house. It can be covered with either a flat glass panel or a plastic dome.

Sliding window: Similar to a double-hung window turned on its side. The glass panels slide horizontally.

Snap-in grilles: Ready-made rectangular and diamond-pattern grilles that snap into a window sash and create the look of a true divided-light window.

Soffit: A boxed-in area just below the ceiling and above the vanity.

Solid-surfacing countertop: A countertop material made of acrylic plastic and fine-ground synthetic particles, sometimes made to look like natural stone.

Space reconfiguration: A design term that is used to describe the reallocation of interior space without adding on.

Spout: The tube or pipe from which water gushes out of a faucet.

Stock cabinets: Cabinets that are in stock or available quickly when ordered from a retail outlet.

Subfloor: The flooring applied directly to the floor joists on top of which the finished floor rests.

Surround: The enclosure and area around a tub or shower. A surround may include steps and a platform, as well as the tub itself.

Task lighting: Lighting designed to illuminate a particular task, such as chopping.

Tone: The degree of lightness or darkness of a color.

Trompe l'oeil: French for "fool the eye." A paint technique that creates a photographically real illusion of space or objects.

True divided-light window: A window composed of multiple glass panes that are divided by and held together by muntins.

Undercabinet light fixtures: Light fixtures that are installed on the undersides of cabinets for task lighting.

Universal design: Products and designs that are easy to use by people of all ages, heights, and varying physical abilities.

Wainscoting: Paneling that extends 36 to 42 inches or so upward from the floor level, over the finished wall surface. It is often finished with a horizontal strip of molding mounted at the proper height and protruding enough to prevent the top of a chair back from touching a wall surface.

Wall cabinet: A cabinet, usually 12 inches deep, that's mounted on the wall a minimum of 15 inches above a countertop.

Xenon bulb: A bulb similar to a halogen bulb, except that it is filled with xenon gas and does not emit ultraviolet (UV) rays. In addition, it is cooler and more energy efficient.

Index

Index

Index

Photo Credits

T: Top R: Right B: Bottom L: Left C: Center

All photography by Mark Samu, unless otherwise noted.

page1: courtesy of Hartco **page 3:** design: Kitchen Dimensions **page 4:** design: Delisle/Pascucci **pages 6–7:** (*TL*) design: Ken Kelly; (*R*) design: Kitchen Dimensions; (*BL*)design: Kitty McCoy, A.I.A. **pages 8–10:** design: Ken Kelly **page 11:** design: Sam Scofield, A.I.A. **pages 12–13:** design: Lucianna Samu/Sunday Kitchens **page 14:** design: Delisle/Pascucci **page 15:** design: Mojo-Stumer, A.I.A. **page 16:** builder: Bonacio Construction **pages 18–19:** design: Rita Grants **pages 20–21:** design: Jim DeLuca, A.I.A. **pages 22–23:** styling: Tia Burns **pages 24–25:** architect: SD Atelier, A.I.A. **page 26:** (*T*) design: Kitchen Dimensions; (*C*) design: Jeanne Stoffer; (*B*) design: Ken Kelly **page 27:** design: Ken Kelly **page 28:** (*T*) courtesy of Hearst Magazines; (*B*) design: Lucianna Samu **page 29:** (*TL*) courtesy of Hearst Magazines; (*TR*) design: Kraft Maid; (*RC*) builder: Witt Construction; (*BL*) builder: Gold Coast Construction **page 30:** (*T*) design: Montlor Box, A.I.A.; (*BL*) design: Sherrill Canet; (*BC*) design: Andy Levtovsky, A.I.A.; (*BR*) design: Habitech **page 31:** design: Patrick Falco **pages 32–33:** (*C, TR, BR*) courtesy of Hearst Magazines; (*BL*) design: Richard Schlesinger; (*TL*) design: Len Kurkowski, A.I.A. **page 34:** (*T*) design: KraftMaid; (*B*) design: Ken Kelly **page 35:** courtesy of Hearst Magazines **page 36:** (*T*) design: Jim DeLuca, A.I.A.; (*B*) builder: Access Builders **page 37:** (*T*) design: Jim DeLuca, A.I.A.; (*B*) courtesy of Hearst Magazines **page 38:** design: Ken Kelly **pages 40–41:** (*C, TR, BC, BL*) design: Ken Kelly; (*BR*) Builder Architect Magazine **pages 42–43:** builder: T. Michaels Contracting

pages 44–47: design: Jean Stoffer **pages 48–49:** (*C, BC, BL, TL*) design: Kitchen Dimensions **page 50:** design: KraftMaid **page 51:** design: Eileen Boyd **pages 52–53:** design: Jean Stoffer **pages 54–55:** design: Patrick Falco **pages 56–57:** styling: Tia Burns **pages 58–59:** design: Ken Kelly **pages 60–61:** (*C*) design: Andy Levtovsky, A.I.A.; (*TR, BR*) design: Bruce Nagle, A.I.A.; (*BL*) builder: Bonacio Construction **page 62:** design: Jim DeLuca, A.I.A. **page 64:** design: Habitech **page 66:** design: Kitty McCoy, A.I.A. **page 67:** builder: Access Builders **page 68:** (*T, BR*) design: Ken Kelly; (*BL*) design: Jean Stoffer **page 69:** (*TR*) design: The Breakfast Room; (*LC*) design: Jean Stoffer **page 70:** (*LC, RC*) design: Kitty McCoy, A.I.A.; (*B*) courtesy of KraftMaid **page 71:** (*L*) design: Ken Kelly; (*R*) design: Kitty McCoy, A.I.A. **page 76:** courtesy of Kraft-Maid **page 77:** (*TR*) design: Mojo-Stumer, A.I.A.; (*BR*) architect: SD Atelier, A.I.A.; (*TL*) design: Habitech **pages 72–73:** (*TC*) builder: Gold Coast Construction; (*TR*) courtesy of Hearst Magazines; (*BR*) design: Montlor Box, A.I.A.; (*BC*) builder: Gold Coast Construction; (*BL, LC, TL*) design: Ken Kelly **page 74:** (*T*) courtesy of Hearst Magazines; (*BR*) design: Ken Kelly; (*BL*) builder: T. Michaels Contracting **page 75:** courtesy of Plain & Fancy **page 78:** (*TR*) courtesy of Plain & Fancy; (*RC*) design: Jean Stoffer; (*BR, BL*) courtesy of Plain & Fancy; (*TL*) courtesy of Hearst Magazines **page 79:** design: Tom Edwards **page 80:** (*T*) design: Delisle/Pascucci; (*BL, BR*) design: Jean Stoffer **page 81:** design: Jean Stoffer **page 82:** courtesy of Plain & Fancy **page 83:** design: Jean Stoffer **pages 84–85:** (*R, BC, BL, LC, TL, TC*) courtesy of Plain & Fancy; (*C*) design: Delisle/Pascucci **page 86:** design: Ken Kelly **page 87:** courtesy of KraftMaid **pages 88–89:** (*C, TR, BR*) courtesy of Plain

& Fancy; (*BC*) courtesy of Miele **page 90:** (*TC, C*) courtesy of Plain & Fancy; (*BR*) design: Mojo-Stumer, A.I.A.; (*BC*) design: Patrick Falco; (*BL*) courtesy of Hearst Magazines; (*LC*) design: Paula Yedyank; (*TL*) design: Lucianna Samu **page 91:** (*TL*) design: Jean Stoffer; (*TR*) design: Ken Kelly; (*BR*) design: Jean Stoffer; (*BL*) design: The Breakfast Room **page 92:** courtesy of Hartco **page 94:** design: Ken Kelly **page 96:** (*TR, BR*) courtesy of Hearst Magazines; (*L*) photo: Don Wong/CH; painting: Dee Painting & Faux Finishes **page 97:** (*TR*) design: Montlor Box, A.I.A.; (*BR*) design: Correia Designs Ltd. **page 98:** (*TR*) design: Patrick Falco; (*B*) courtesy of Glidden; (*TL*) design: Sherrill Canet **page 99:** courtesy of Sherwin Williams **pages 100–101:** (*BR*) builder: Bonacio Construction; (*TC, TL*) design: Ken Kelly **page 102:** (*TR*) builder: T. Michaels Contracting; (*B*) design: Paula Yedyank; (*TL*) design: Jean Stoffer **page 103:** design: Eileen Boyd **page 105:** (*T*) design: Andy Levtovsky, A.I.A.; (*BR, BL*) courtesy of Thibaut **page 106:** courtesy of Armstrong **page 107:** (*TL*) architect: SD Atelier, A.I.A.; (*B*) courtesy of Armstrong **page 108:** (*R*) courtesy of Robbins; (*L*) Brian C. Nieves/CH **page 109:** (*T*) design: Ken Kelly/Carpen House Cabinets; (*B*) courtesy of Robbins **pages 110–111:** (*TC*) courtesy of Crossville; (*BR*) design: Correia Designs Ltd.; (*BL*) courtesy of Crossville **page 112:** design: Ken Kelly **page 113:** design: Kitty McCoy, A.I.A. **pages 114–117:** courtesy of Armstrong **page 118:** design: Kitty McCoy, A.I.A. **page 119:** (*T*) courtesy of Above View; (*BR, BL*) courtesy of Armstrong **page 120:** courtesy of Hearst Magazines, design: Val Florio, A.I.A. **page 122:** (*R*) design: Habitech; (*BL*) design: Andy Levtovsky, A.I.A.; (*TL*) design: Ken Kelly **page 123:** (*TR*) design: Mojo-Stumer, A.I.A.; (*BR*) courtesy of Maytag; (BLC) courtesy of Whirlpool; (L) courtesy of GE **page 124:** (TL) design: Ken Kelly; (BL) builder: Access Builders **page 125:** (TR, RC, BR) courtesy of GE; (BL) builder: Access Builders; (TL) design: Ken Kelly **pages 126–127:** courtesy of Wolf **page 128:** (TR) courtesy of Sharp; (BR, BL) design: Ken Kelly; (TL) courtesy of Wolf **page 129:** (L) courtesy of Wolf **page 130:** (TL) courtesy of KraftMaid; (BR) builder: Witt Construction; (BL) courtesy of Hearst Magazines **page 131:** (TR) design: Paula Yedyank; (B) courtesy of Wolf; (TL) design: Montlor Box, A.I.A. **page 132:** (TL) courtesy of Wolf; (BL) design: Delisle/Pascucci **page 133:** (TL, TR) design: Jean Stoffer; (BR) design: The Breakfast Room; (BL) builder: Access Builders **page 134:** (TL, TR) courtesy of GE; (BR) courtesy of Sub-Zero; (BL) courtesy of Kenmore **page 135:** architect: SD Atelier, A.I.A. **pages 136–137:** (TLC, TRC) design: Kitty McCoy, A.I.A.; (BR) courtesy of Sub-Zero; (BC) courtesy of GE; (L) design: Jean Stoffer **page 138:** (TL, RC) design: Jean Stoffer; (BL) design: Courland Design **page 139:** (TL, TR) courtesy of Sub-Zero; (B) courtesy of Big Chill **page 140:** (TL) courtesy of GE; (TR) design: Courland Design; (BL) courtesy of Jenn-Air **page 142:** (TL) courtesy of Hearst Magazines; (TR) design: Ken Kelly; (BR) courtesy of Fisher & Paykel **pages 142–143:** courtesy of Fisher & Paykel **page 144:** (T) courtesy of Maytag; (BR) courtesy of Whirlpool; (BC, BL) courtesy of Miele **page 146:** bulder: Access Builders **page 148:** design: Jean Stoffer **page 149:** design: Ken Kelly **page 152:** (TL, TR) courtesy of Moen; (BL) courtesy of Blanco **page 153:** (BR) courtesy of Moen **pages 154–155:** (TC) design: Mojo-Stumer, A.I.A.; (R) design: Ken Kelly; (BC) design: Jean Stoffer; (L) courtesy of Sonoma **page 156:** courtesy of Kohler **page 157:** (T) courtesy of

Kohler; (BR, BL) courtesy of Wilsonart **pages 158–159:** (TC, TR) design: Kitchen Dimensions; (RC) design: Ken Kelly; (BR) courtesy of Elkay; (BL) design: Kitchen Dimension; (TLC) design: Kitchen Dimensions **page 160:** courtesy of Kohler **page 161:** (TL) courtesy of Sonoma; (TR) courtesy of Wilsonart; (B) courtesy of Kohler **page 162:** (T) design: Ken Kelly; (B) courtesy of Delta **page 163:** (T) design: Andy Levtovsky, A.I.A.; (B) courtesy of Watermark **page 164:** (TL) courtesy of Moen; (BR) design: Ken Kelly; (BL) builder: Bonacio Construction **page 165:** (T) design: Lucianna Samu; (B) courtesy of Hearst Magazines **page 166:** (TL) courtesy of MGS; (TR) design: Patrick Falco; (B) courtesy of Moen **page 167:** (TL) design: Habitech; (TR) courtesy of Hearst Magazines **page 168:** (TR) builder: Access Builders; (BR) design: Jean Stoffer; (L) courtesy of MGS **page 169:** (T) courtesy of Moen; (B) design: Lucianna Samu **page 170:** (L) courtesy of Moen; (TR, RC) design: Ken Kelly; (B) design: Lucianna Samu **page 171:** (BL) courtesy of Moen; (TR) design: Kitty McCoy, A.I.A. **page 172:** design: Jean Stoffer **pages 174–175:** (T) design: Granite & Marble Works; (BR) design: Kitchen Dimensions; (BRC) courtesy of Hearst Magazines; (BLC) painting: InPaint Workshops & Studio; furniture: Choice Seating; (L) design: Eileen Boyd **pages 176–177:** courtesy of Zodiaq **pages 178–179:** (TC) courtesy of Formica; (R, BR, BL) courtesy of Corian; (TL) design: Ken Kelly **page 180:** (T, TR) courtesy of Crossville; (BR, BL) design: Ken Kelly **page 181:** (B) courtesy of Daltile **pages 182–183:** (TR, BR, BL) design: Ken Kelly; (LC) design: Walker Zanger; (TL) design: Ken Kelly **pages 184–185:** courtesy of Formica **page 186:** (T) courtesy of DEX Studios; (B) courtesy of Sonoma **page 187:** (T) courtesy of Hearst Magazines; (BL) courtesy

of Sonoma; (BR) **pages 188–189:** (TC) design: Jean Stoffer; (BR) courtesy of Just Manufacturing; (BC) courtesy of Hearst Magazines; (TL) design: Sam Scofield, A.I.A. **page 190:** design: Andy Levtovsky, A.I.A. **page 192:** (T) design: Patrick Falco; (B) architect: SD Atelier, A.I.A. **page 193:** design: Eileen Boyd **pages 194–195:** (TR) design: Kitty McCoy, A.I.A.; (BR) design: Len Kurkowski, A.I.A.; (BC) architect: SD Atelier, A.I.A.; (BL) courtesy of Zodiaq **pages 196–197:** (TL) design: Correia Designs Ltd.; (R) courtesy of Rejuvenation; (BR) Correia Designs Ltd. **pages 198–199:** (T) design: Ken Kelly; (bottom row) design: Jean Stoffer **pages 200–201:** (TL) design: Ken Kelly; (TR) design: Delisle/Pascucci; (BR) design: Andy Levtovsky, A.I.A.; (BL) courtesy of Hearst Magazines **page 202:** (T) design: Kitchen Dimensions; (B) courtesy of Hearst Magazines **page 203:** (TL) design: Paula Yedyank; (TR) design: Ken Kelly; (BR) design: Lucianna Samu/Granite & Marble Works **page 204:** (T) design: Lucianna Samu; (B) design: Tom Edwards **page 205:** (TL) design: Ken Kelly; (TR) courtesy of Hearst Magazines; (BL) design: Rita Grants

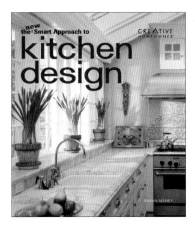